Talking About

Information & Communication Technology

in Subject Teaching

GW00702368

A guide for:

Student Teachers

Mentors

Tutors

KS3 & KS4

SECONDARY

Canterbury Christ Church
University College

First published in 1998 by:

Canterbury Christ Church
University College
North Holmes Road
Canterbury, Kent, CT1 1QU

● ●

Production team

Editor and co-ordinator:
Phil Poole

Editorial consultant:
Tristram Shepard

Design, illustration and production:
Tristram Ariss

Photographs and electronic imaging:
Richard Bentley

This publication is Canterbury Christ Church University College's response to the initiative by the Teacher Training Agency (TTA) to equip providers of Initial Teacher Training to deliver the new standards for Information and Communication Technology (ICT) in subject teaching.

Canterbury Christ Church University College would like to thank the tutors, student teachers, mentors and its partnership schools who have contributed in so many ways to the development and production of this publication.

Canterbury Christ Church University College contributors

Mike Blamires
Peter Dorman
Phil Everitt
Kit Field
Chris Fisher
Derek Greenstreet
Richard Harris
Rita Headington
Simon Hughes
Will Katene
Andrew Lambirth
Elizabeth Marsden
Chris Philpott
Phil Poole
Stephen Scoffham
William Stow
Tony Turner
Jo Westbrook
Viv Wilson

Partnership schools

John Alexander
Angela Ayling
Lesley Johnson
Theresa Kennedy
Shalley Lewis
Roz Morton
Ros Newington
Louise O'Sullivan
Mary Pottinger
John Rivers
James Seal
Jim Smith
Ann Snailham
Carol Webb
Brian White
Ben Williams
Liz Willis

Student teachers

Richard Bentley
Peter Elliott
Candice Hambridge
Phil Horstrup
Robert Picton
Philip Quinn
James Wheeler

Other contributions

Debbie Green
Robert Easton
Alison Page
Tristram Shepard

Editing

Sarah Ware

Printing

Parkers Printing, Canterbury

Acknowledgments

Featherby Junior School, Gillingham

St. Peter's Methodist Primary School, Canterbury

Rainham Mark Grammar School

The Westlands School, Sittingbourne.

The authors would like to acknowledge the contribution of BECTa materials, in particular their:

- Software reviews
- CD-ROM reviews
- Information sheets
- Approaches to IT capability

The Standards for the use of ICT in subject teaching are drawn from DfEE (1998) Teaching: High Status, High Standards. Circular 4/98

SIR, Systems and Integrated Research (Integrated Learning Systems), for their screen-shots.

Windows screen-shots are reprinted with the permission of Microsoft Corporation.

ISBN 1–899–253–45–9

98 99 00 01 02 / 10 9 8 7 6 5 4 3 2 1

Contents

We live, it is often said, in interesting times. One of the things that makes these times particularly interesting is that we are living on the edge of major transition from one type of society to another, from an industrial age to an information and communication age. Just as the factory and the potential of mass-production shaped the nineteenth and twentieth centuries, the microchip and the potential of mass-communication will shape the new millennium in ways which are still difficult to imagine and predict.

The information age will bring major changes to the way in which we live our daily lives, be it at work, how we shop, the provision of health–care or our entertainment and leisure. It will also have a profound effect on the way we learn, and how we are taught.

To prosper in the twenty-first century will require new skills and capabilities, and new ways of thinking about things. Not only do we need to know how to use information and communication technology, we need to know when to use it, and, indeed, when not to use it. As teachers of the very first generation who are growing up within the information age, we have a responsibility to prepare these children as best we can for the sorts of lives they are likely to lead.

To meet this challenge, teachers will need to rely not only on the computer or the latest digital satellite video links, but also on something much more familiar – our skills in communicating with each other through ordinary, everyday conversation. It will be by talking (and of course listening) to each other in an informed, purposeful way that we will begin to explore the issues of how and when to use information and communication technology appropriately and effectively in our teaching and learning.

This book is intended specifically to help mentors, student teachers and tutors to talk to each other about the issues involved in the use of information and communication technology (ICT) in schools. It aims to provide a starting point and focus for discussion as they begin to shape and form the learning experiences of the future.

'By 2002 all schools will be connected to the Superhighway, free of charge; half a million teachers will be trained [to teach with ICT]; and our children will be leaving school IT-literate, having been able to exploit the best that technology can offer.'

Tony Blair, 1997

New standards

The Government's aspirations for dramatically improving the use of Information and Communication Technology (ICT) in education were clearly expressed in the above introduction to *Connecting the Learning Society*, The National Grid for Learning (1997).

One of the first manifestations of a new initiative was the announcement of new standards for the use of ICT in subject teaching, which all NQTs must achieve. The new standards are set out in Circular 4/98, *Teaching: High Status, High Standards*. From September 1998 these standards will determine the content of courses that initial teacher training providers and their partnership schools deliver.

The emphasis of the new standards is on effective teaching with ICT in subject teaching, which applies to *all* student teachers who are expected to understand the nature of ICT and its role in learning, and to be able to plan for effective classroom use. Also identified are a range of knowledge and associated skills with ICT which the course has to provide for those student teachers who do not already have them.

The standards set for new teachers from 1998 will also ultimately be those for all existing teachers. The Government has announced an ambitious four-year programme focused on the ICT capability of all teachers. In exemplifying the standards for newly qualified teachers, this publication also aims to provide a resource that will be of use to all teachers in partnership schools.

Mentors, teachers, tutors and student teachers have collaborated to produce these support materials to help partnerships meet the challenge of developing student teachers' ICT capability. Copies of this publication are being circulated to all Canterbury Christ Church University College mentors and tutors as well as the student teachers.

To tie in with this publication there is a World Wide Web site based at Canterbury Christ Church University College, called DISTRICT (Distance Information to Support Training in ICT) **http://www.cant.ac.uk/district**. The site is also linked to further support materials and resources on the Internet. Together, this publication and the Web site offer a set of resources to support the attainment of the new standards.

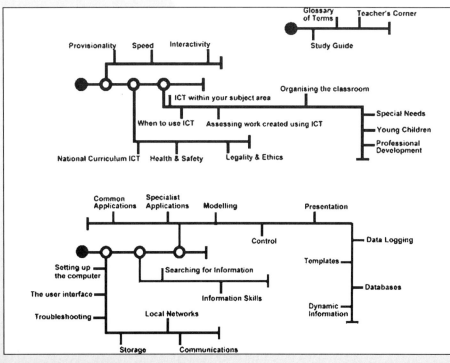

Using these materials

The publication encapsulates some of the main features and issues associated with areas of the TTA standards. It does not provide a complete course in ICT. In the limited space available it is not possible to offer the detailed support needed to gain many of the practical skills in ICT that most student teachers will require. These will partly be met through college-based sessions and peer-support, together with the DISTRICT Web site which contains an important section on 'Common applications'. This section contains 'on-line' tutorials on the most common computer applications such as *Microsoft Word* and *Access*, E-mail and the use of the Internet. In the future, working from 'on-line' resources will be an important skill for all teachers.

On most pages the appropriate TTA standards are shown in the top left-hand corner. These may not always be fully exemplified on the page. Relevant links to other pages are therefore indicated in the bottom right. These will need to be followed to obtain a more complete picture of the knowledge, skills and understanding required.

It is hoped that the publication and the Web site will be used as a point of contact and the basis for a working dialogue between student teacher, mentor and college tutor. The materials provide a starting point for discussion, and a checklist for use when reviewing progress throughout the course of training.

Section One: Mentoring and planning

The first section offers a number of strategies for successful management of ICT resources in classroom and computer suites. Lesson planning techniques and essential preparation to enable teachers to be successful in their use of ICT are outlined.

Section Two: Teaching with ICT

This section deals with some of the pedagogic issues surrounding the use of ICT to support learning in all curriculum subject areas. It does not attempt to be definitive, prescriptive or to teach particular aspects of ICT. It offers information that student teachers, mentors and tutors can share as they develop their use of the technology.

Section Three: ICT skills

The final section is primarily about the knowledge and understanding of ICT that is required to successfully use the hardware and software, both professionally to support assessment and the preparation of learning materials, and in the classroom.

> Descriptions of practice in schools within the text occasionally include the names of specific items of software. These are used as examples and do not imply recommendation.

What are the main concerns of mentors and student teachers regarding ICT? Here a mentor and a student share different perceptions of their experiences.

A mentor's perspective

As a mentor I face a range of challenges in my role within the partnership between college, student and school. In terms of supporting the development of my students' ICT competences some of the key roles I play are concerned with:

- *matching of class, teacher and student ICT skill level and experience*
- *providing access to appropriate hardware and software*

As a mentor I have expectations of my students. They need to take the initiative in terms of:

- *sorting out the problems of everyday operation of ICT resources themselves*
- *being flexible in working with ICT resources which may be different to those found in college, possibly out-of-date, or sometimes more up-to-date*
- *assisting other teachers in the use of ICT resources*
- *sharing planning of ICT work and its documentation in schemes of work*
- *sharing college materials with me and the class teacher*
- *making examples of good practice available to the school*
- *carrying out an ICT audit of the school for their own information*
- *knowing the health and safety practices of the school in regards to ICT.*

I also have expectations of the College. For example, I rely on:

- *access on a regular basis to examples of good practice*
- *access to ICT course details in simple format*
- *certain items of kit to supplement the school's resources*
- *access to college prepared materials, e.g. worksheets, software and assessment material.*

As in all curriculum areas, mentors want students to use and develop their ICT teaching skills. It is important to ensure ICT is planned and executed on the teaching practice. There is often a danger that ICT is left out or simply added on for pupils as a reward or time-filler.

Don't be put off by a dusty relic in the corner of the classroom, and an anti-ICT teacher. When staff see you succeed, they might change their view and might even learn something from you. Remember, pupils love to use ICT and can often be motivated by using the computer, particularly when they are often denied its use.

A student teacher's perspective

The majority of ITT students bring with them some experience and skill in the area of Information Technology. They begin the course with a variety of ICT skills but more importantly, motivation to further their IT capability. Throughout the course they have access to ICT facilities and tutorials in college and school, and most importantly the encouragement to implement their skills in the classroom.

My initial concerns for incorporating ICT into my teaching practice were classroom management and planning issues. For example:

- *How many computers were available for the lesson, and how would this affect pupils' work, class set-up, group and individual work?*
- *What expectations should I set for the pupils?*
- *What did I need to know about ICT classroom management strategies?*
- *How was the ICT room set up for teaching? Could this be changed? Were there any computers in the department?*
- *How should I plan for the diversity of pupils' ICT skills?*

- *Did pupils have a timetabled ICT lesson where they were taught keyboard and other skills?*
- *What software packages were available at school and which were the pupils familiar wi[...]*

I needed to do some research into the IT Department, its status within the school and other departments, and whether my mentor and the other teachers I was working with would be able to give me guidance on when it was best to use ICT in connection with my subject area. I was also interested to discover what IT skills the teachers in my own department had.

After employing ICT during my teaching practice a new set of issues arose. For example:

- *What is available for instructing and focusing the class as a whole, i.e. is there a screen projector or whiteboard that the whole class can see?*
- *Are there printers available so that pupils can hand their work in at the end of the lesson, and is the printing facility fast enough to make the ICT lesson effective in terms of assessment and the meeting of targets?*

- *Is the ICT lesson teacher-led or a pupil-centred learning environment: can I realistically and effectively help all pupils or do I set up groups/pairs and seating in such a way that pupils can support each other's learning?*
- *How do I ensure that my aims and objectives, planning and practice rely on effective teaching strategies so that learning outcomes are successful and fulfilling?*

And most importantly, am I making ICT support the subject-specific aims and requirements of the National Curriculum?

I thoroughly enjoyed the subject-ICT challenge in my ITT year and feel well equipped to tackle the new ICT requirements. However, there are another new set of concerns for me as I enter my NQT year:

- *What are the school's ICT policies and politics and how do they plan to tackle the new ICT initiatives?*
- *Will the IT Co-ordinator be supportive?*
- *How will the school utilise the National Grid for Learning?*

- *What and where can I get funding for developing ICT resources in my school and subject area?*
- *What INSET is there for developing skills and raising the status of ICT within my school?*

This final question is a crucial one. I have found that many teachers are not aware or interested in the teaching and learning benefits of ICT within their subject area. How will I be able to exploit the technology if the attitude of colleagues is negative? Until the attitudes of many teachers changes markedly these ICT fruits will go un-reaped.

Standards

7

Trainees must be taught how to contribute to the development and consolidation of pupils' ICT capability within the context of the subject being taught through:

a. explicit discussion and, where necessary, teaching of the ICT skills and applications which are used in the subject;

b. using ICT terminology accurately and appropriately, and explaining to pupils any ICT terminology which arises from the application of ICT to the subject;

c. using ICT in ways which provide models of good practice for pupils, and insisting that pupils employ correct procedures when using applications.

16

Trainees must demonstrate that they:

a. know and understand the ICT requirements of the pupils' National Curriculum in relation to the phase(s) and subject(s) to be taught;

b. are familiar with the standards as set out in the pupils' National Curriculum for IT, relevant to the phase for which they are training to teach, and know the level of IT capability they should expect of pupils when applying ICT in the subject(s).

'IT is to ICT as literacy is to books, journals or screen displays. The focus of IT is on pupils' capability with ICT. For this reason IT is the title used for the national curriculum subject qualifications.'

QCA (1998)

Teachers who are not specialists in the use of Information and Communication Technology in the curriculum may find understanding the various demands for the use of ICT in schools perplexing:

- What is the relationship between IT and ICT?
- What is expected of me as a classroom teacher?
- Who delivers what?
- What does the IT co-ordinator do?
- What does the IT department do?
- What is the experience of the pupils?

What are Information and Communication Technologies (ICTs)?

ICTs are the computing and communications facilities and features which variously support teaching, learning and a range of activities in education. These could include:

- media materials such as TV, video and radio resources
- micro-computers
- peripherals such as alternative access tools, interfaces for control and sensing equipment
- Internet access and use
- integrated learning systems   (ILS)
- video conferencing facilities
- electronic mail systems
- electronic toys
- electronic assessment and recording systems.

What is Information Technology (IT) capability?

Information Technology (IT) comprises the skills, knowledge and understanding needed to employ Information and Communication Technology (ICT) appropriately, securely and fruitfully, in learning, employment and everyday life.

At a statutory level all state schools have an obligation to provide a programme of study which meets the requirements of the Order for Information Technology (IT). Levels of attainment are set for IT as for other curriculum subjects. The National Curriculum Programme of Study for IT capability has two main components:

- Communicating and handling information
- Controlling, monitoring and modelling

IT capability is characterised by an ability to use effectively IT tools and information sources to analyse, process and present information, and to model, measure and control external events.
This involves:

- using information sources and IT tools to solve problems
- using IT tools and information sources, such as computer systems and software packages, to support learning in a variety of contexts.
- understanding the implications of IT for working life and society.

As pupils make progress they are expected to use ICT in a more purposeful way, and to become more critical and autonomous, learning for themselves when it is appropriate to use, and not to use, ICT.

Communicating and handling information

This strand provides the mainstay of a pupil's IT experiences, permeating activities across most subjects of the curriculum and providing situations where many of the opportunities outlined in the first part of the Programme of Study can be developed.

Communicating information

This is the area of IT with which most teachers are familiar, including, as it does, the most frequently encountered use of computers: word processing. However, word processing is not the totality of this area and teachers may also need to seek out opportunities for pupils to use graphics, music programs, multimedia authoring and presentation packages, E-mail and the Internet.

Handling information

This is often thought of as the 'database and spreadsheet' strand but is actually much more. It is only when pupils have some understanding of how to sort and classify information, real or imagined, that they can begin to understand what the software can do. Teachers should provide opportunities for pupils to develop these concepts in a variety of situations.

Controlling, monitoring and modelling

Control

Pupils should look at how everyday objects are controlled using IT and will be developing sequences of commands for controlling floor robots, screen images and external devices. This also relates to the use of technology in music.

Monitoring

Pupils can use sensors attached to computers to measure changes in light, temperature, movement or sound.

Modelling

Pupils need to acquire an early awareness of computer modelling through the use of simple adventure programs where the rules and objectives are defined clearly. Pupils can make limited decisions within the confines of rules determined by the author, but will be unable to alter the rules governing the outcomes. Later, using simulation or modelling software, pupils will be able to ask 'What would happen if....?' type questions and change rules governing various outcomes.

Standards

7

Trainees must be taught how to contribute to the development and consolidation of pupils' ICT capability within the context of the subject being taught through:

a. explicit discussion and, where necessary, teaching of the ICT skills and applications which are used in the subject;

b. using ICT terminology accurately and appropriately, and explaining to pupils any ICT terminology which arises from the application of ICT to the subject;

c. using ICT in ways which provide models of good practice for pupils, and insisting that pupils employ correct procedures when using applications.

16

Trainees must demonstrate that they:

a. know and understand the ICT requirements of the pupils' National Curriculum in relation to the phase(s) and subject(s) to be taught;

b. are familiar with the standards as set out in the pupils' National Curriculum for IT, relevant to the phase for which they are training to teach, and know the level of IT capability they should expect of pupils when applying ICT in the subject(s).

'All teachers need to be aware of the nature of pupils' IT competence because everyone who uses the technology with pupils contributes to their developing competence and has expectations of it when they teach with ICT.'

ICT in subject teaching

The Teacher Training Agency (TTA) developed the standards for newly qualified teachers (NQTs) which appear throughout this publication. These are contained in the document 4/98 *Teaching: High Status, High Standards*, DfEE (1998). The standards for ICT in subject teaching sit alongside those for Mathematics, English and Science, together with a number of general requirements. The standards apply to all NQTs and are targets for *them* to achieve, not for the pupils.

The standards apply to all NQTs because the Government's objective is to empower teachers to exploit the new technologies to support their teaching, whatever their curriculum speciality. The focus of the standards is on the subject being taught and aspects of organisational administration rather than the direct development of pupils' knowledge, skills and understanding with ICT.

How will it work in school?

The new ICT in subject teaching initiative seeks to clarify and promote good practice which already occurs in some subjects and some schools to make it a more formalised and effective part of pupils' experience.

There are a number of approaches which schools currently adopt. In some schools the IT co-ordinator and the staff in their department take overall responsibility for delivery of the IT National Curriculum. Pupils have specific regularly timetabled lessons where the objectives are to raise pupils' levels of achievement in the various aspects of IT. Ideally these place activities in the context of other curriculum subject areas, such as English, Mathematics and Science, but their subject objectives are not always their prime focus. With this system, subject teachers need to be aware of the developing IT capability of their pupils so that they can set subject-specific tasks which further inform and build on what they can do already.

In other schools delivery is exclusively through the schemes of work of each department. As well as meeting the requirements of their own Programmes of Study a department will ensure that pupils also cover the requirements of a particular aspect of the IT requirement. Many schools successfully adopt a combination of these two approaches, with a programme of IT-specific lessons, supported by a number of key subject departments.

Whatever the approach, two things emerge as being critical to success. The first is the quality of the day-to-day planning, co-ordination, monitoring and evaluation of pupils' exposure to IT in terms of progression, continuity and differentiation. The second is that the school senior management team and the governors have articulated a clear vision of IT in the school and are seen to be active in supporting its development.

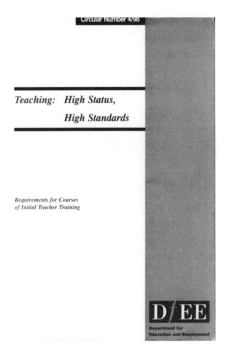

Circular Number 4/98

Teaching: **High Status,**
High Standards

*Requirements for Courses
of Initial Teacher Training*

Information Technology

in the National Curriculum

D/EE
Department for
Education and Employment

WELSH OFFICE   England and Wales

DfE
DEPARTMENT FOR
EDUCATION

Who are they?

DfEE (The Department for Education and Employment.)

QCA (The Qualifications and Curriculum Authority) is the statutory body which has responsibility for the implementation of the National Curriculum for IT. Its focus is on the curriculum provision in schools.

The Teacher Training Agency (TTA) is responsible for the standards of teachers emerging from initial teacher training courses and the continued professional development of teachers in schools.

What will pupils' experience be?

Throughout Key Stage 3 the curriculum will need to be planned so that all pupils progress in all aspects of IT. At the end of the Key Stage pupils' levels of attainment will be assessed against the NC levels and be reported to parents. During Key Stage 4 pupils should be expected to continue to make further progress within the context of the GCSE courses. There will be optional examination courses in IT at GCSE, GNVQ and A-level. Across the curriculum, pupils should find more coherent opportunities to use ICT in each subject area.

What will be expected of teachers?

All subject teachers will increasingly be expected to make appropriate and effective use of ICT resources to deliver their subject objectives. This will be supported by INSET which will be potentially available to all teachers. Some teachers will also have responsibilities to deliver the IT objectives as well. In particular, teachers need to be able to strike an effective balance between encouraging the development of pupils' critical, autonomous use of ICT and the need for the systematic teaching of skills and delivering good practice in relation to IT capability.

What do teachers need to know?

Teachers will need:

- knowledge and understanding of effective teaching methods using ICT
- to know how to assess subject objectives when pupils use ICT
- a sound grasp of the technologies themselves as they relate to teaching and administration
- an understanding of the National Curriculum for IT
- data about pupils' levels of IT capability.

It is necessary for teachers to have a working knowledge of the IT National Curriculum Order to enable them to understand how the ICT they use will contribute to the development of pupils' IT Capability. To enable teachers to plan effectively they will also need to be aware of the level at which pupils are operating so that they can provide appropriate tasks and resources to move pupils' IT capability forward.

It would be unwise for a student teacher to assume that every computer is the same and that all schools have the same computers as the college. This is unlikely to be the case, although the situation is steadily getting better! It is important to find time to talk with the IT co-ordinator in order to discover the range and type of equipment and the facilities available for use.

There may well be a considerable gulf between the resources of the college and schools. It is likely that many schools will have less sophisticated hardware and will not run the same type or as great a variety of software. It is therefore vital to ensure that any work planned in college can actually be carried out in schools. However, some schools are well equipped in specific areas (e.g. video-conferencing) that the college is not currently providing.

Many students will find that they are more confident in the use of ICT than their mentors. As such they will often need to take the lead in ensuring the school is able to support them fully in achieving their ITT competences. The mentor or class teacher will, however, still need to play an important role in providing access to resources and in supporting the development of classroom resource management skills.

Human resources

- Who is the IT co-ordinator or manager?
- Who has the technical skills to put things right when they go wrong? For example, is there a technician or network manager?
- Will classroom support be available during lessons?

How is IT organised?

- What IT skills can pupils be expected to have in each year?
- What hardware will they be confident with?
- How familiar will they be with the particular software to be used?
- Does the subject area contribute formally to the development of pupils' IT capability?

Hardware and software

- What hardware is available in the school and where is it located? (Mac/PC, peripherals, etc.)

- Does the school have a network? If so, can the computers also be used as stand-alone machines? (This is an important issue if the network should crash during a lesson, for example.)

- What main software packages are used by the school? Are these the same as those used in college? Are they the same versions? If not, are the versions backwards compatible? (Don't produce files in college or school, only to find that these cannot be used in the other establishment.)

- What operating systems are in use? Bear in mind that some schools may still be using Windows 3.1.rather than Windows '98, '95 or NT,

- Does the school's software support long file names, or will they be truncated, causing confusion?

- What will happen if printers go wrong (a common problem)? How can paper be un-jammed?

- How can it be ensured that any floppy discs are formatted correctly and at the right density? (Have some spare, clean discs available for saving material in an emergency.)

Security

- Will an ID and password be needed to access the network or individual computers?

- How much access is allowed to the network system?

- Will it be possible to upload software applications or files, so that a whole class can access the same file through the network, or will the network manager have to do this? Beware of falling foul of the copyright legislation by using software which is only licensed for a single or limited number of users.

Access

- Does the school operate a booking policy for its ICT rooms? If so, where is the booking sheet?

- Are pupils allowed into rooms unsupervised?

- Do rooms have to be unlocked/locked? If so, where is the key?

- Can the floppy disc drives be accessed? Are pupils allowed to download files to use at home/upload files from home?

Standards

3

For those aspects of lessons where ICT is to be used, trainees must be taught to identify in their planning:

a. the way(s) in which ICT will be used to meet teaching and learning objectives in the subject;

b. key questions to ask and opportunities for teacher intervention in order to stimulate and direct pupils' learning;

c. the way(s) in which pupils' progress will be assessed and recorded;

d. criteria to ensure that judgements about pupils' attainment and progress in the subject are not masked because ICT has been used;

e. any impact of the use of ICT on the organisation and conduct of the subject lesson and how this is to be managed;

f. how the ICT used is appropriate to the particular subject-related objectives in hand and to pupils' capabilities, taking account of the fact that some pupils may already be very competent. and some may need additional support.

The most successful lessons that use ICT will be the best planned lessons. The teacher needs to be clear about the intended outcomes of the lesson with regard to the content. The pupils need to be clear about what they are going to do, how they are going to do it and what they are going to use it for.

Lesson planning

Written lesson plans make explicit teachers' objectives and the organisational strategies for achieving them. Additionally they also identify assessment and evaluation techniques necessary to monitor effectiveness of the teaching and learning.

Before planning:

An audit will yield important information on which to base planning decisions.

- The number of machines available (stand-alone, networked?)
- The level of support from technician or IT co-ordinator
- Where the pupils are in terms of their IT capability and their experience with the particular resources involved in the lesson
- The printing facilities there will be
- The rules the pupils work by
- How pupils access the resources and their files

It is essential to make time to become familiar with the software and hardware systems? Try out the activity well before the lesson and make a note of any ICT skills which may be needed. Never assume that the pupils will have these.

Objectives

Teachers need to be clear why they are planning to use ICT within their lesson. They should write down their objectives and clarify in what way using ICT will enable them to achieve these. It is important to check how familiar the pupils are with the computers and the software that will be used in the lesson. Ensuring the equipment will be available when needed is, of course, also essential.

Are the objectives clear for planning to use ICT within the lesson?

- Write down the subject objectives to be delivered
- Identify those objectives that using ICT will help deliver
- What particular benefits of ICT are being utilised?
- What aspects of pupils' IT capability is being used in the lesson?
- What is the potential for extending pupils' IT capability?

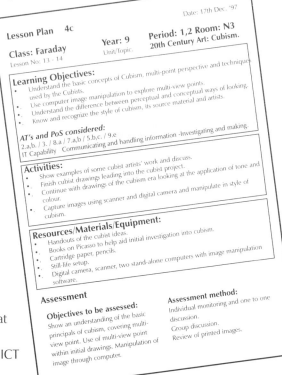

Date: 17th Dec. '97

Lesson Plan   4c

Class: Faraday   **Year: 9**   **Period: 1,2 Room: N3**
Lesson No: 13 - 14   Unit/Topic.   20th Century Art: Cubism.

Learning Objectives:
- Understand the basic concepts of Cubism, multi-point perspective and techniques used by the Cubists.
- Use computer image manipulation to explore multi-view points.
- Understand the difference between perceptual and conceptual ways of looking.
- Know and recognize the style of cubism, its source material and artists.

AT's and PoS considered:
2.a,b. / 3. / 8.a / 7.a,b / 5.b,c. / 9.e
IT Capability   Communicating and handling information -Investigating and making.

Activities:
- Show examples of some cubist artists' work and discuss.
- Finish cubist drawings leading into the cubist project.
- Continue with drawings of the cubism era looking at the application of tone and colour.
- Capture images using scanner and digital camera and manipulate in style of cubism.

Resources/Materials/Equipment:
- Handouts of the cubist ideas.
- Books on Picasso to help aid initial investigation into cubism.
- Cartridge paper, pencils.
- Still-life setup.
- Digital camera, scanner, two stand-alone computers with image manipulation software.

Assessment

Objectives to be assessed:
Show an understanding of the basic principals of cubism, covering multi-view point. Use of multi-view point within initial drawings. Manipulation of image through computer.

Assessment method:
Individual monitoring and one to one discussion.
Group discussion.
Review of printed images.

Assessment

What methods of recording will be used to monitor pupils' access to limited resources such as a stand-alone computer in the classroom? Which lesson objectives for the subject and IT capability will be assessed? How will the outcomes of pupils' efforts be assessed? Will there be concrete outcomes such as print-outs?

Planning the activity

Anticipate that whatever activity is planned will always take longer. One lesson is never enough to type up a story! It is always worth trying out the activity well before the lesson and make a note of any specific ICT skills which may be needed. Never assume that all the pupils will have these.

Differentiation

However the class is grouped, streamed or setted there will a wide diversity of IT capability within it. It is essential to have tasks which can stretch the most able and support those that require more support. Worksheets or Web-based tasks can allow pupils to work at their own pace and provide tutorial support to reinforce direction given by the teacher. Tasks where pupils can determine the type of outcome they are working towards will inevitably offer greater scope for differentiation and a raised level of motivation, e.g. the report on an Internet research session is presented as a poster, or brochure, PowerPoint presentation or a Web page.

The unexpected

Plan an alternative activity to replace the ICT element of the lesson, e.g. an alternative to searching the Times CD can be searching a photocopied front page of a newspaper for given information. Expect that printers will be a problem!

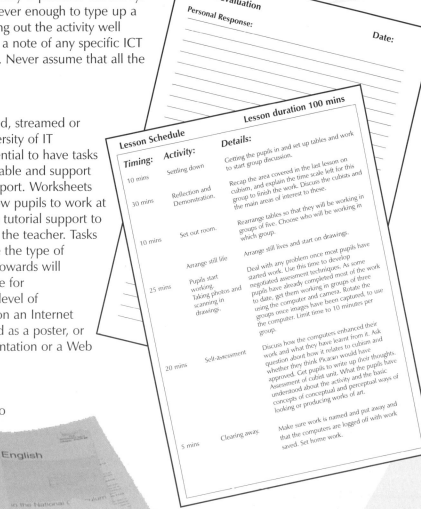

Resource areas

If pupils are to visit a resource area, such as the library, to access ICT resources will they:

- know the software they are intended to use?
- know the rules about access to the machine?
- manage the task within the time allocated for each group?
- use verbal written or on-line guidance to support them?
- have the schedule for groups available for them to see?
- be able to have access to any additional support in the resource area?

Further information

Auditing available resources
Objectives in the use of ICT
Managing ICT in the classroom
Mentors and students talking
Legal and ethical issues
Health and safety

Standards

4

Trainees must be taught the most effective organisation of classroom ICT resources to meet learning objectives in the subject, including how to:

a. use ICT with the whole class or a group for introducing or reviewing a topic and ensuring that all pupils cover the key conceptual features of the topic;

b. organise individuals, pairs or groups of pupils working with ICT to ensure that each participant is engaged, that collaborative effort is balanced, and that teacher intervention and reporting back by pupils takes place where appropriate;

c. make ICT resources available to pupils for research or other purposes which may arise either spontaneously during lessons or as part of planned activity, ensuring that the resource is used profitably to achieve subject-related objectives;

d. position resources for ease of use, to minimise distraction, and with due regard to health and safety;

e. ensure that work done using ICT is linked to work away from the screen, allowing ICT to support teaching rather than dominate activities.

> *Taking your first lesson with a class using ICT can be a traumatic experience for an unprepared teacher. But a successful experience will quickly bring you back for more!*

Using ICT resources in a classroom or network room demands a particular set of classroom management strategies and approaches.

Preparing for the lesson

Student teachers should try to arrange to observe an experienced colleague using ICT with a class or group. The lesson does not need to be in their specialist subject as the principles and good practices of using ICT are transferable.

Introducing the task

Make the focus of the lesson clear at the outset (ideally prime the class in the previous lesson). Avoid using generic terms without giving a clear explanation, e.g. 'We're going to do multimedia.' Pupils may have no concept of what multimedia is, so it is better to say 'Today we're going to combine words, sound and video to create an interactive storybook. This is called a multimedia presentation.'

Will pupils be drafting directly to screen or working from hand drafts already produced? Given a choice between the computer and paper pupils will nearly always use the PC. If drafting to paper is required first, try to arrange for this to be done for homework or in a previous lesson. Ideally maximise the use of the machines while you have the resource.

Demonstrations

Giving a short demonstration to show the outcome of the activity is common practice. How will this be done? Does the school have a large monitor or data projector so that all pupils can see what you are doing? If the pupils are grouped around you, how many will be able to see at any one time?

Give only a few instructions at a time. You may need to give several demonstrations during the lesson. Some pupils will find it difficult to follow mouse movements on the screen: this is a kinesthetic experience and cannot be acquired by observation. Back up instructions with worksheets or key points on the board.

Classroom and pupil management

Be aware that different rooms have different layouts for the PCs, so expect that pupils will be facing the wall in many IT rooms! This will change the way in which the group behaves and responds to the teacher. An issue for teachers can be a loss of voice effectiveness, because they will invariably have their backs to some students. There may also be a loss of control of the group, who may become unclear what the 'classroom rules' now are. These need to be established at the outset. One clear rule that needs to be established is: 'When I want to talk, everyone takes their hands off the keyboards and listens', and when pupils are using multimedia: 'When I want your attention I would like you all to take off your headphones'. The teacher needs to insist that the rules are adhered to.

Find the best place to group the class together if lengthy instructions or explanations need to be given out. Pupils will become very distracted if the teacher tries to talk to them seated at the computers. Normal classroom protocol still applies, e.g. 'Hands up'. The class can degenerate into calling out 'Miss, Miss' and eventually walking round the room in search of help. This happens particularly if the class is unclear of the activity or if the IT skills required are too complex for the pupils. A successful lesson will have few hands up. Worksheets to reinforce the skills required for a successful outcome will help reduce the constant need for help and reassurance with ICT.

Using laptops and/or stand-alones within the subject classroom

How do teachers enable all pupils to have access to ICT resources when there are more pupils than computers? The class teacher will act as a guide and indicate what access arrangements the pupils are familiar with and who has/has not used the computer yet. Many teachers organise their classroom so that two pupils work together on a computer, allowing for collaborative work and discussion. This requires organisation to keep track of which pupils have had access to the resources. A record in a mark book is useful!

With small networks collaborative group working, using a pair of computers, is possible, e.g. one pair of pupils open the word processor and record the progress and edit a report of the discoveries made. e.g. 'Investigate pyramids', the second pair of pupils access the Internet sites provided as bookmarks.

It may well be that ICT access is staggered throughout the year. Some pupils may use ICT in a module of work, while others use more traditional methods.

What will the rest of the class be doing whilst the computer is in use? Preparation, drafting and planning before accessing the computer will save a great deal of wasted computer time. The outcome will be more productive the more prepared the pupils are to use the computer.

Keep the tasks short and realistic. The timing of the task is important and there are no easy answers. It will always take longer than anticipated. Pupils' IT capability will show a spread of levels which you will need to allow for. Set appropriate targets – 'I would like you to finish entering your data by...', 'I would like a print out by the end of today's lesson and remember to put your name on the page please.' Some pupils will take a great deal longer than anticipated. Decide when the cut off point will be. Can you allow the pupils to continue beyond the end of the particular unit of work?

There may be gender issues. Girls may be far more reluctant and prefer to use pen and paper and generally write copiously. Boys on the other hand will often readily volunteer to use the computer and be keen to show off their skills but may not be particularly productive. Some guidance and encouragement will be needed.

Differentiation

What will the pupils do who finish the computer task early?
How will you support the slower workers to achieve a satisfactory outcome for them?

Ending the lesson

Allow enough time for saving, logging off, collecting folders, tidying the room, etc. This will need at least five minutes. Make arrangements for collecting printouts still in the print queue after the end of the lesson.

Stand-alones
- Are these password protected?
- How should peripherals such as printers, concept keyboards or interfaces be connected?
- Is the required software on the machine?
- How will groups or individuals be organised to access the machine(s)?

Networks
- Do all pupils have a user ID and passwords?
- How does the school deal with these?
- Are the user IDs and passwords to hand for the class?
- Are any temporary user IDs available if pupils' passwords, etc. fail?
- What will those pupils do who cannot log on?
- What will happen if the equipment fails during the lesson?
- Are there different user interfaces e.g. one room may use Windows '95, another Windows 3.1?
- Are there different versions of a software application, e.g. Word 2.0, Word 6.0, Word '97?
- Pupils may need to access their work from a different drive.

Dealing with printing
How can printers be accessed through the software? Try this out and be clear what the steps are. One of the most problematic areas of classroom management can arise at the end of the lesson with queues of pupils at the printer:
- Insist as a classroom rule that pupils remain in seats and do not gather around the printer.
- Allow time for printing. All too often the last instruction in the lesson is 'Print your work'. This causes havoc. Printing needs to begin at least 15 minutes before the close of the lesson. (Watch out for large graphics files, they take longer to print.)

Further information
Auditing available resources
Objectives in the use of ICT
Lesson planning
Mentors and students talking
Legal and ethical issues
Health and safety

Standards

1

Trainees must be taught how to decide when the use of ICT is beneficial to achieve teaching objectives in the subject and phase, and when the use of ICT would be less effective or inappropriate. In making these decisions, trainees must be taught how to take account of the functions of ICT and the ways that these can be used by teachers in achieving subject teaching and learning objectives. This includes:

a. how the **speed and automatic functions** of ICT can enable teachers to demonstrate, explore or explain aspects of their teaching, and pupils' learning, more effectively;

b. how the **capacity and range** of ICT can enable teachers and pupils to gain access to historical, recent or immediate information;

c. how the **provisional nature** of information stored, processed and presented using ICT allows work to be changed easily;

d. how the **interactive way in which** information is stored, processed and presented can enable teachers and pupils to:

   i. explore prepared or constructed models and simulations, where relevant to the subject and phase;

   ii. communicate with other people, locally and over distances, easily and effectively;

   iii. search for and compare information from different sources;

   iv. present information in ways which are accessible in different forms for different audiences.

Trainees should be taught what the implications of these functions are for achieving teaching objectives in the relevant subject(s). However, trainees must be made aware when pupils' skills in mental or written calculation are not being developed and therefore the activity may not suit the particular teaching objectives in hand.

Using ICT brings many benefits, particularly in terms of pupil-motivation. Speed, automation, capacity and range, revision and interactivity further increase productivity. These gains are not achieved over-night, however, and teachers need to be patient and persistent in the development of innovation in the classroom.

There are many enthusiastic IT teachers in education and a newcomer can easily feel intimidated when they meet the 'expert'. In reality, although they may have made a good start, very few teachers have yet managed to integrate fully the use of ICT into their normal teaching practice.

In the short term ICT will probably increase a teacher's workload within a curriculum that is already perceived as overcrowded. Despite the considerable potential benefits, classroom management, technical issues, instructional and pupil monitoring problems will in many cases weigh heavily against the high pupil and teacher interest in using ICT.

It is important that a teacher's early experiences in using ICT in teaching are positive. Unsatisfactory attempts, where objectives are ill-informed and resources unreliable, can be counter-productive. Teachers are pragmatists: they are willing to try new ideas, but quickly abandon those that are unreliable or unsuccessful.

What are the benefits of ICT?

ICT can be categorised in terms of its:

- speed and automatic functions: monitoring, controlling and feedback
- capacity and range: richness of resources, the power of communications
- provisionality: ease of amending the outputs
- interactivity: dynamic feedback and immediate response to changing inputs.

Speed and automatic functions

Collecting large amounts of data and processing it rapidly are tasks that computers are very good at. Automatic collection of measurements from electronic sensors is one of the functions of sensing equipment. This has particular relevance to curriculum areas such as Science, Geography and PE.

Automatic control systems can be created from a range of electronic sensors and output devices such as motors, lights, loudspeakers, etc. Control functions feature strongly in design and technology and music. Automatic functions are also of great use in integrated learning systems (ILS) where monitoring a pupil's answers automatically provides the most appropriate learning route.

The graph plotting capability of spreadsheets allows pupils to examine quickly a number of ways of displaying data, allowing them to look for patterns without having to re-plot the data manually.

Graphics and CAD packages allow design ideas to be developed quickly.

Capacity and range

This feature is concerned with the diversity of ways in which information can be presented, the ability to communicate with people all over the world and the immediacy of the availability of information. Information on the Internet is up-to-date, sometimes to the minute, and can bring life to research into current issues better than traditional reference resources.

Provisionality

Work can be revised easily with ICT. For pupils working to extend their literacy skills or prepare a presentation this is an important feature. Word processors can be thought processors, allowing ideas to be revised without the chore of a total re-write. A number of applications can take the tedium out of traditional methods of working and open up opportunities for higher-order thinking, such as interpretation. Art and Music software encourages experimentation without the fear of losing what has already been created.

Interactivity

The interactive way in which information can be processed and presented enables teachers and pupils to:

- explore prepared or constructed models and simulations
- communicate with other people, locally and over distances, easily and effectively
- search for and compare information from different sources
- present information in ways which are accessible in different forms for different audiences.

Motivation

The motivational aspect of using computers seems to be generally accepted, as long as ICT tasks are set appropriately. ICT can provide a safe and non-threatening environment for learning. This allows pupils to make mistakes, to go back over their work and to move at their own pace without holding up others. The most advanced learning systems offer instant feedback and learning experiences that are geared to the pupil's stage of development in a particular aspect of a subject. Many pupils find the provisional nature of ICT applications allows them to correct mistakes and progressively develop their ideas.

Able pupils find the scope of ICT liberating and enjoy exploring new ideas at their own pace. The capacity and range of material can challenge all pupils, whatever their ability.

The speed and automatic functions of ICT allow teachers to bring experiences into the classroom that would have been unthinkable a few years ago. For example, searching for the use of a particular word or phrase throughout the works of Shakespeare can take just seconds!

ICT offers a different range of features which pupils find motivating and teachers perceive to be useful. Teachers of different subjects will find particular features more appropriate than others.

Does IT work?

Firm evidence for the effectiveness of computers in teaching and learning is difficult to find in educational research literature. However, case studies abound, full of anecdotal evidence about the value of ICT in the classroom. Despite the organisational difficulties that ICT undoubtedly creates, positive experiences of teachers continue to motivate teachers and pupils alike.

Standards

2

Trainees must be taught how to use ICT most effectively in relation to subject-related objectives, including:

a. using ICT because it is the most effective way to achieve teaching and learning objectives, not simply to motivate pupils or as a reward or sanction for good or poor work or behaviour;

b. avoiding the use of ICT for simple or routine tasks which would be better accomplished by other means;

c. knowing that, where ICT is to be used, appropriate preparation of equipment, content and methodology is required;

d. avoiding giving the impression that the quality of presentation is of overriding importance and supersedes the importance of content;

e. structuring pupils' work to focus on relevant aspects and to maximise use of time and resource,

f. having high expectations of the outcomes of pupils' work with ICT, including:

   • expecting pupils to use ICT to answer valid questions appropriate to the subject matter being taught;

   • when appropriate, requiring pupils to save work, and evaluate and improve it;

g. making explicit the links between:

   i. the ICT application and the subject matter it is being used to teach;

   ii. ICT and its impact on everyday applications.

Teachers need to consider when the use of ICT will benefit the teaching of their subject and the development of pupils' IT capability as required by the National Curriculum for IT. The objectives set out in lesson planning should clearly indicate the gains in subject terms and in IT capability, where appropriate.

Pupils' IT capability can be enhanced when work with ICT allows:

• subjects to provide good contexts for pupils to apply IT skills

• the creation of presentations for a range of audiences appropriate to the subject material

• pupils independently to envisage that their work will be improved by using a computer and appropriate software.

Before planning a lesson it is useful to ask the following questions:

• How could ICT develop the learning of particular knowledge or skills within the subject?

• How might ICT free the learner from low-level tasks to participate in higher order thinking?

• How might ICT encourage pupils to ask questions and engage in problem solving activities?

• How might ICT enhance and enrich the educational experiences of pupils?

• What IT skills will be required and which could be developed?

As teachers begin to use ICT with classes, many go through a phase of concentrating on the presentation of written work or drill and practise learning exercises. These are not challenging for the pupils or the teacher but can be useful to establish basic rules and for the teacher to gain confidence. The challenge for teachers is to develop activities which exploit the benefits of ICT while not inhibiting other important achievements in the subject.

For example:

• A single-sided word processed document with no pictures and the default font will do nothing to enhance either the subject material or the IT capability of the pupil. A bi-fold leaflet with selective use of fonts and illustration, showing a clear design for the audience, will set higher standards of achievement.

• Removing the tedium from graph-plotting using the graphing capability of spreadsheet applications will not be appropriate if the objective is to teach basic skills about setting scales on two axes or plotting points.

• Spending time searching the Internet may be inappropriate when introducing a new idea to a whole class, whereas it may enrich a pupil's experience when individually researching a particular project.

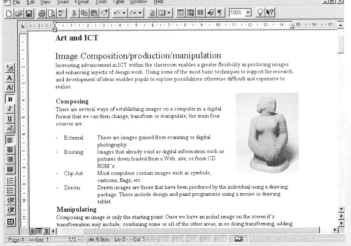

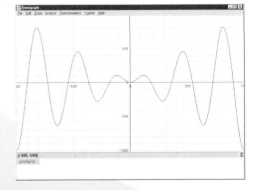

Below are two examples of the successful use of ICT:

Subject:	Geography
Topic:	Field trip
Task:	Drawing beach/cliff profiles for a classroom display.
Objectives:	Drawing beach/cliff profile using a spreadsheet Measuring on site Using a ruler and pencil to measure accurately
Differentiation	
for some:	Creating an accurate profile of the beach/cliff
for all:	Producing a neat and clear diagram
for all:	Presenting for an audience
Sequence:	Pupils take measurements and heights in the field and return to classroom. Pupils use suitable software: spreadsheet with graphing function, word processing
IT capability:	Pupils use suitable presentation techniques for wall display and achieve level 6/7 NC IT

Subject:	Maths
Topic:	Investigating exterior angles and polygons
Task:	Pupils have been taught that there is a relationship between the exterior angle of a polygon and the number of sides. Pupils are to investigate the exterior angles for a range of shapes.
Objectives:	Calculating the exterior angle Reinforcing long division Reinforcing times-tables Understanding that exterior angle = 360/ no. of sides
Suitable software:	Spreadsheet, *Logo*, graphical geometry software.
IT capability:	This activity will allow pupils to show off their skills at modelling. Creating procedures - developing logical skills Changing variables Pupils will be modelling at level 6 NC for IT

When not to use ICT

- To simply enhance the look of written material - pupils' IT skills are undervalued and unused.
- Tasks are too trivial for ICT use and not thought through — we'll use a computer today to …
- Insufficient planning leaves ICT as an add on — objectives for subject and use of ICT are not clearly defined.
- ICT becomes the prime focus and subject content becomes secondary to the task.

Further information

ICT & IT capability
Lesson Planning
The Benefits of ICT in subject teaching
Literacy and ICT
Numeracy and ICT
Assessing the use of ICT

Teaching with ICT

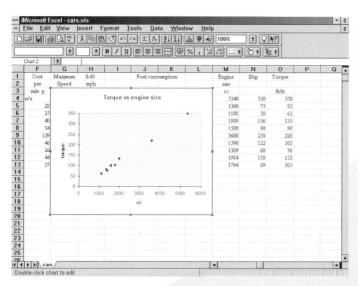

The National Literacy Strategy defines literacy as 'the ability to read and write', but it also encompasses speaking and listening. It naturally contributes to the National Curriculum for English, but also sets an agenda for all teachers.

The Literacy Strategy sets out the objectives under three strands:

- Word level
- Sentence level
- Text level.

Literacy is relevant to teaching across the whole curriculum, in particular where the focus is on reading and writing non-fiction texts.

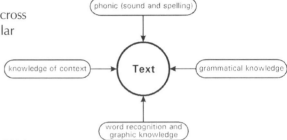

Writing for different audiences can be motivating when it uses computers:

- constructing a World Wide Web page
- a multimedia presentation
- a rolling presentation for the foyer using a presentation package
- an item for a class database of reviews.

Computers can give pupils a chance to achieve where they have previously failed.

- Pupils who have difficulty with handwriting can be encouraged to express themselves using a word processor. With confidence it is more likely that they will wish to improve their handwriting
- Changes can be made easily allowing experimentation
- Spell checkers can identify those words which pupils continually find difficult and so help them improve the quality of their writing
- Integrated learning systems (ILS) can support the acquisition of basic literacy skills.
- Multimedia authoring allows pupils to construct exciting pages to explore text. Sounds, video, graphics, clip art and animated sequences can all be achieved from a simple suite of tools.
- Experienced writers can use the word processor to develop the structure of stories, and to draft and redraft their work. Planning layout can be supported using on-screen writing frames.

Assessing literacy gains

An area of concern for teachers generally is the assessment of pupils' work when it is ICT based, for example a reading, spelling or information processing/organising task. To overcome these potential obstacles try to ensure:

- that pupils have the facility to print out their work or
- they save it to an accessible disk or drive
- that the package the pupils are using has a facility that records what pupils have done
- that the work has a context outside the ICT skills or packages that can be assessed.

"Towards a new definition of Literacy

IT holds a central position within the curriculum because, as well as being a subject in its own right, the technology is a means through which learning can be achieved. If we consider the phrase 'read with confidence, fluency and understanding' it is embellished with richer connotations within the context of ICT. Pupils should be able to 'read' words, images, sounds, icons, and symbols at word and sentence level, as well as interactive and intertextual texts 'with confidence, fluency and understanding'. Thus, 'interest in books' extends to all kinds of ICT texts: electronic, multimedia, interactive, collaborative and the 'texts' of the Internet which fuse a variety of texts, genre and media.

In using ICT formats and templates in their writing, pupils will become 'familiar with some of the ways that narratives are structured', and will 'understand and be able to use and create a range of non-fiction texts'. For example, the use of an application such as *Microsoft Publisher* can offer pupils a set of templates in which to construct their work for a particular audience. Through informed use of spell and grammar checks pupils will be able to 'plan, draft, revise and edit their own writing'. Using many of the ICT resources and educational software, pupils will be 'able to orchestrate a full range of reading cues (phonic, graphic, syntactic, contextual) to monitor and self-correct their own reading', and will 'have an interest in words and word meanings, and a growing vocabulary' and will 'understand the sound and spelling system and use this to read and spell accurately'.

Subject-specific ICT vocabulary can be introduced through exploration of the topic in terms of the pupils' experiences and knowledge before or as they arise, and is part of the process of acquiring literacy skills. Many ICT texts and tasks require pupils sifting, skimming, and scanning through texts as well as reading aloud, receptive, shared and guided reading.

ICT formats, templates and forms provide pupils with access to different genre, formats, presentational aspects and use of sound and images that allow development in writing. Through ICT writing can easily be collaborative, shared, manipulated and passed between pupils, classes and countries. It is in this spirit and manner that ICT challenges traditional definitions of the scope of literacy.

As teachers we seek to educate pupils for a life that consists of cash-dispenser monitors, home-shopping, the Internet, as well as an underlying emphasis on the importance of the availability and speed of information and services at the touch of a touchpad, a keyboard or a telephone panel. Not only do pupils have to be able to read, write and communicate through language, they must be able to comprehend, interpret and manipulate the meaning of icons, symbols, language, sounds and interactive texts that are part of ICT literacies. The world has been made even smaller by the advent of E-mail and video-conferencing. The World Wide Web has saturated the globe with information in a time-period that could not have been predicted. 'Edu-' and 'info-tainment', computer games, hand-held digital cameras with accompanying editing and printing facilities, home-shopping, Internet chatlines, school Websites, and the idea of multimedia texts that exploit sound, images, including audio-visual ones, music, and text-based technologies that are collaborative and self-managed processes of handling information, are all facets of everyday life for school pupils today.

The new drives for Literacy within education are seeking to address the relationship between ICT literacies and National Curriculum literacies. The prospect of a National Grid for Learning essentially means that literacy has encompassed ICT within its scope. With a new set of literacies must come a re-definition of Literacy.

ICT has provided pupils with the chance to become involved in a culture of collaborative and interactive creation. ICT opens an exciting and intertextual world of sound, text and image. Pupils must be equipped with the skills of speaking and listening, reading and writing within the context of ICT: if they are not, how can they communicate and participate in all aspects of twenty-first Century life? "

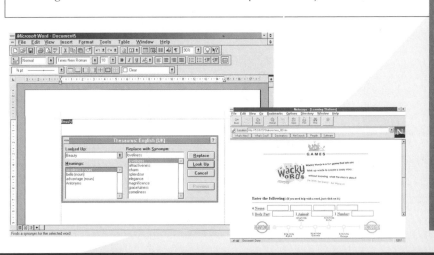

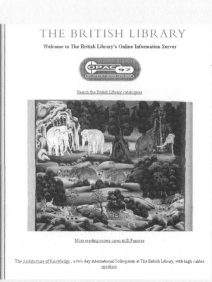

Numeracy at Key Stages 1 and 2 is a proficiency that involves a confidence and competence with numbers and measures. It requires an understanding of the number system, a repertoire of computational skills and an inclination and ability to solve number problems in a variety of contexts. Numeracy also demands practical understanding of the ways in which information is gathered by counting and measuring, and is presented in graphs, diagrams, charts and tables.

DfEE (1998)

While secondary schools have expectations of primary schools teaching the basics of numeracy there is still plenty of work to do at secondary level. Numeracy, alongside literacy, is a vital access tool to other curriculum areas. If a teacher expects pupils to handle numbers, estimate, order, calculate, use money, measure, handle data and display it in graphs and charts, handle shape, symmetry, position and direction, then they are contributing to pupils' numeracy skills.

National Numeracy Strategy (NNS)

This initiative is built on the work of the National Numeracy Project. Its objective is to raise the standards of numeracy. While its main focus is on primary education there are implications for secondary provision to build on the foundations laid for them. At Key Stage 3 there will still be a number of pupils working at levels below the average for their age who will need support throughout the curriculum as well as specific help from the mathematics department.

The framework for teaching mathematics at primary level has a greater emphasis on oral work and mental calculation but it also covers the introduction of formal written calculation methods. It sets out teaching objectives, year upon year, showing how to pace work so that the emphasis is on acquiring numeracy skills as well as other mathematical principles. By 1999 the strategy will be in place in primary schools.

Numeracy across the curriculum

- In Geography pupils use co-ordinates, bearing and direction, collect data and then present it.
- In History they create time lines, collect data and present it in a graph, chart or table.
- In Art they look for symmetry, shapes and patterns.
- In Science they collect data by measuring physical quantities, then analyse and display it using a variety of strategies. They make estimations and calculate.
- In Physical Education they measure distance, speed and time, and perform calculations.

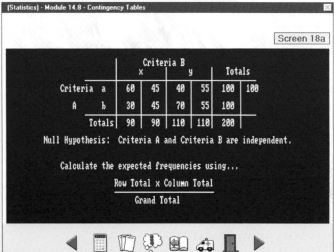

How can ICT support numeracy?

The DfEE suggests that particular types of software (and hardware) may be especially valuable:

- that enable teachers to introduce and develop specific aspects of number, to sharpen pupils' mental recall and calculation skills
- that teachers can use for demonstrations with large groups, for example to zoom in on graphs and charts
- that pupils can use to practise and extend what is taught in class for those who need more time for consolidation
- that enable pupils to practise number system concepts enjoyably.

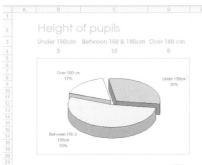
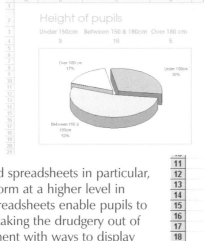

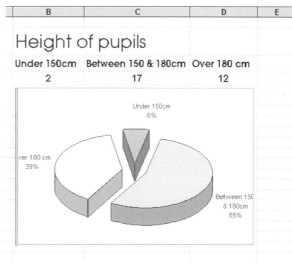

Spreadsheets

Many of the subject specific pages in this publication illustrate the way in which ICT, and spreadsheets in particular, can enable pupils to perform at a higher level in number-related work. Spreadsheets enable pupils to handle number work by taking the drudgery out of data handling, to experiment with ways to display information, to look for patterns and to learn how to employ them as labour saving tools. This does not mean that they do not need to have a sound grasp of number operations. Setting up a spreadsheet to perform an operation automatically and display the results effectively challenges most adults! Modelling with spreadsheets demands a high level of numeracy and mathematical skills.

Calculators

Most pupils should be proficient users of a calculator by the time they enter secondary school. In addition to Mathematics, calculators offer support for pupils in subjects such as Science, Geography and History by allowing pupils to gather data collected in experiments and research, which will often contain numbers which make mental calculation difficult. Whenever possible pupils should be encouraged to make simple calculations without reference to a calculator. Pupils should be encouraged to make order of magnitude mental approximations whenever possible. Using the calculator's memory to store values whilst undertaking calculations is a skill that will feed into effective use of spreadsheets for analysing data.

Graphical calculators are blurring the distinction between computers and calculators. Hand-held computers are putting calculator and computer software capability in the hands of teachers and pupils. It is important that the functions of these devices are used against a background of basic numeracy.

Graphical and design applications

Graphical and computer aided design (CAD) packages will reinforce pupils' grasp of 2D and 3D shapes, symmetry, co-ordinates, position, movement and direction.

Control applications

Instructions and sequence are at the heart of writing control sequences. In music and design and technology pupils are practising their mental agility in estimating, place value and ordering. The instant feedback of changes to number or ordering, such as the movement of a lift or the playback from a synthesiser, is highly motivating.

Integrated learning systems (ILS)

In many secondary schools integrated learning systems (ILS) are being used to teach aspects of numeracy and mathematics. If teachers are involved in using aspects of numeracy in their curriculum area they should acquaint themselves with the strategies and style of teaching employed in these systems to enable them to build on this foundation. Evaluation evidence indicates that the school context in which these systems are operated is one of the most significant factors in their effectiveness.

Internet resources

The National Grid for Learning (NGfL) will contain many ideas and strategies for employing ICT in relation to subject teaching, many of which will be based around aspects of numeracy. Teachers around the world are contributing ideas for exciting lessons in areas of numeracy and mathematics. The BBC and the GCSE examinations boards have created some popular Web sites where pupils can revise (or learn) concepts in mathematics using interactive worksheets.

NRICH is an internet site from which teachers of very able pupils in mathematics can download support materials.

Further information

The benefits of ICT in subject teaching
SEN and ICT
ICT in Mathematics
Flexible learning resources
Using spreadsheet software
Using graphic software
Using the Internet

Standards

5

Trainees must be taught to recognise the specific contribution that ICT can make to teaching pupils with special educational needs in mainstream classrooms based upon the need to:

a. provide access to the curriculum in a manner appropriate to pupils' needs;

b. provide subject-specific support.

15

Trainees must demonstrate that they are aware of the potential of ICT to enable them to prepare and present their teaching more effectively, taking account of:

a. the intended audience, including matching and adapting work to subject matter and objectives, pupils' prior attainment, reading ability or special educational needs; recognising the efficiency with which such adaptations can be made using ICT;

b. the most appropriate forms of presentation to meet teaching objectives,

A child in your class may have learning difficulties caused by:
- *a physical disability;*
- *a problem with sight, hearing or speech;*
- *a mental disability;*
- *emotional or behavioural problems;*
- *a medical or health problem;*
- *difficulties with reading, writing, speaking or mathematics work;*

ICT has the potential to add flexibility in applying required strategies for addressing identified needs. The skill is in making time to consider how strategies can be applied with an individual learner within the constraints of the classroom and the school.

Legally a child has special educational needs if he or she has learning difficulties and needs special help. This help is known as special educational provision. A child has learning difficulties if he or she finds it much harder to learn than most pupils of the same age, or if he or she has a disability which makes it difficult to use the normal educational facilities.

How can ICT support provision for SEN?

The Code of Practice recommends that for each child's special needs, the potential benefits of ICT should be explored and then access to appropriate resources should be secured alongside appropriate training for the child and the staff involved.

Sally Paveley (1997) suggests that ICT may be useful in helping with particular areas of need.

Pupils with a Physical Disability

ICT may be essential for access for some pupils

ICT can help with written work

Regular assessment, training and support is needed for pupils and helpers to ensure equipment is suitable

ICT Resources
- Communication aids
- Computer access devices - switches, adapted mice, keyguards
- Access utilities and specialised software
- Software with alternative input options
- Word list and word prediction facilities

Pupils with a Visual Impairment

Pupils may need help to make the most of their vision when using ICT, e.g.,
- consider the position of the pupil
- consider the position of the screen
- consider the clarity of the display
- use large, clear fonts if they help
- adjust the colours
- add speech feedback where possible

ICT Resources
- Talking word processors
- Big pointer utilities
- Screen magnifiers
- Screen readers
- Electronic Braillers
- Closed circuit television

Pupils with Hearing Impairments

Where Language is a major problem:
- ICT can be used for language development activities
- symbol or picture enhanced text can bring meaning to print
- illustrated overlays make writing more accessible using a 'concept keyboard'.
- access to whole words can aid expression and help pupils to organise their ideas
- graphics can stimulate writing

ICT Resources
- Symbol generating software
- Word processors
- Overlay Keyboards
- Word lists
- Clip art to illustrate writing
- Spell checkers and grammar checkers

The Code of Practice is a guide for schools and LEAs about the practical help they can give to pupils with special educational needs. It recommends that schools should identify pupils' needs and take action to meet those needs as early as possible, working with parents. The Code gives guidance to schools but it does not tell them what they must do in every case.

To use ICT effectively
- Be aware of the range of needs of the pupils you teach.
- Be aware of the targets that any pupils with Individual Education Plans (IEP.s) have
- Differentiate teaching to take account of needs and targets
- Monitor any progress made (involving the child and any available LSA with this)

Things to do
- Make sure you are aware how SEN may be addressed using ICT.
- Review existing SEN software and devices in the school.
- Highlight differentiation possibilities with ICT in schemes of work.
- Prepare some vocabulary lists on a word processor for each key stage.
- Find out how ICT is being used to support the SEN policy within the school.
- Consider how ICT can support Individual Education Plans(IEPs).
- Discover what advice/help can be obtained from the LEA /Advisors/ Consultants/Internet sites on specific issues.

Pupils with Specific Learning Difficulties
ICT can be used to support learning and for programmed learning in basic skills

ICT Resources
- Talking books
- Overlay Keyboards
- Word list facilities
- Spell checkers
- Predictors
- Laptop computers
- Talking word processors
- Speech Recognition

Pupils with Learning Difficulties
ICT can:
- be a focus for language development activities
- offer a medium for differentiated activities
- make writing more accessible
- make information more accessible
- enable pupils to practise skills

ICT Resources
- Talking books
- CD-ROMs with good sound and graphics with clear layout and structure
- Drill and practise programs
- Overlay Keyboards
- Word list facilities
- Talking word processors

Pupils with Emotional & Behavioural Difficulties
ICT
- is motivating
- is not threatening or judgmental
- can make tasks more manageable
- can provide satisfying outcomes

ICT Resources
- Multimedia
- Educational 'games'
- Concept Keyboards
- Word list facilities
- Word predictors
- Spell checkers

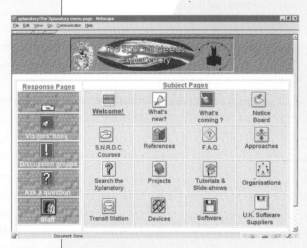

The Special Needs Xplanatory at Canterbury Christ Church University College

Further information
Literacy and ICT
Numeracy and ICT
Alternative input devices
ICT and Flexible Learning Resources
Health and Safety

Teaching with ICT

Standards

2

Trainees must be taught how to use ICT most effectively in relation to subject-related objectives, including:

a. using ICT because it is the most effective way to achieve teaching and learning objectives, not simply to motivate pupils or as a reward or sanction for good or poor work or behaviour;

b. avoiding the use of ICT for simple or routine tasks which would be better accomplished by other means;

c. knowing that, where ICT is to be used, appropriate preparation of equipment, content and methodology is required;

d. avoiding giving the impression that the quality of presentation is of overriding importance and supersedes the importance of content;

e. structuring pupils' work to focus on relevant aspects and to maximise use of time and resource;

f. having high expectations of the outcomes of pupils' work with ICT, including:

· expecting pupils to use ICT to answer valid questions appropriate to the subject matter being taught;

· when appropriate, requiring pupils to save work, and evaluate and improve it;

g. making explicit the links between:

   i   the ICT application and the subject matter it is being used to teach;

   ii ICT and its impact on everyday applications.

17

Trainees must demonstrate that they know how each of the following is relevant to the specialist subject and phase for which they are training:

a. **generic procedures and tools**, including:

   i   understanding the key features and functions used within the subject;

   ii using ICT to prepare material for pupil use.

b. **reference resources**, including;

   i   how to search reference resources;

   ii how to incorporate the use of reference resources into teaching.

c. **the ICT specific to the subject;**

d. the major teaching programs or "courseware" to ensure that material is matched to the pupils' competences.

Word processors, multimedia authoring packages and the Internet provide a wide range of exciting opportunities for pupils to develop their skills in all aspects of English.

Writing/composing texts

The computer should be used as a tool alongside pen and paper. It encourages new ways of thinking and encourages revision while texts are being created.

Pupils can write stories and poems, and choose a lettering style and graphic image to link the content and theme to the audience. The word-count facility can be used to help write mini-sagas of exactly 50 words to focus pupils' choice and economy of words.

Groups can write different scenes to construct a class play. The text can then be passed around the class by E-mail for editing and revision by other groups.

When using integrated learning systems (ILS) to develop basic skills the daily computer print-out of individual pupil needs can be incorporated into mainstream lessons through spelling tests, using words in the context of stories and poems, and other language work.

Presenting texts for particular purposes and audiences

Non-literary pieces such as recipes, pamphlets, letters, memos and agendas can be created on the computer, encouraging pupils to focus on language, images, form, audience and context.

Templates create professional looking news pages and aid the study of tabloid and broadsheet newspapers, contrasting fonts, layout, margins, lengths of paragraphs and sentences, representation and language.

Persuasive adverts and posters can be created using word processing, graphics packages and photos linked to the class reader or poetry.

Multimedia authoring packages enable pupils to consider how texts are read and written in linear and non-linear forms.

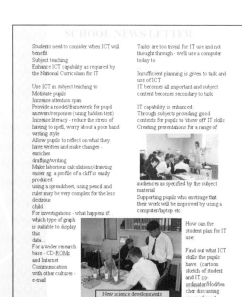

Reading texts

Partially revealed 'cloze' procedure poems and stories, especially the first chapters of books, can be read closely in small groups and the deep structure brought to life. Scratch pads can be used as tools for reflective thought: other pupils can interact with and redraft these texts.

Newspaper articles, images, pamphlets and adverts from CD-ROMs and the Internet can be analysed closely and altered though deletion, substitution, cut and pasting and segmenting, leading to the re-arranging of whole paragraphs, re-shaping and re-sequencing to alter the meaning and message.

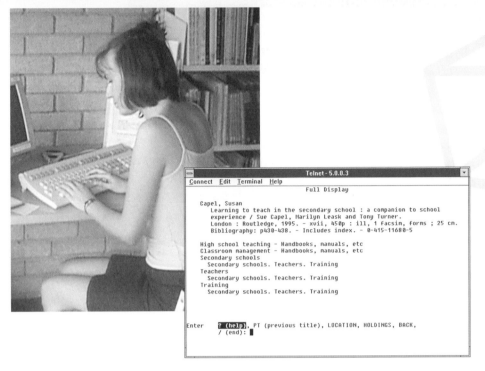

```
                          Telnet - 5.0.0.3                              ▼
 Connect  Edit  Terminal  Help
                         Full Display

 Capel, Susan
      Learning to teach in the secondary school : a companion to school
      experience / Sue Capel, Marilyn Leask and Tony Turner.
      London : Routledge, 1995. - xvii, 450p : ill, 1 facsim, forms ; 25 cm.
      Bibliography: p430-438. - Includes index. - 0-415-11680-5

 High school teaching - Handbooks, manuals, etc
 Classroom management - Handbooks, manuals, etc
 Secondary schools
    Secondary schools. Teachers. Training
 Teachers
    Secondary schools. Teachers. Training
 Training
    Secondary schools. Teachers. Training


 Enter     ? (help), PT (previous title), LOCATION, HOLDINGS, BACK,
           / (end): ▮
```

When to use IT

- When lesson objectives require pupils to focus on presentational devices and particular formats, e.g. FrontPage, agendas and memos.
- For revising and redrafting work where a computer will enhance both the process and the product, e.g. a less able pupil composing and redrafting a letter to be sent to an author on the class reader.
- When enhancing research skills using the Internet and databases following on from using the library resources, e.g. encyclopedia and information books.

When not to use IT

- Shorter pieces of text can be scrutinised on screen; longer bits of text such as extracts, novels, stories are better read in hard, paper copy, especially for less able readers.
- When using a pen to create text allows for a close, tactile writing process.
- When transfer to a word processor does not involve any development.

Questions for teachers

- Who will teach pupils keyboard skills?
- How can we keep boys and girls on-task, considering separate strategies in the use of ICT and talk?
- How can we assess pupils in speaking, listening, reading and writing when they use IT in English lessons?
- How will pupils be influenced by non-standard English found on the Internet and used in E-mails?
- How can differential planning and teaching be tackled in the context of the ICT classroom?

Searching for, retrieving and processing information

The Internet can be used for specific research topics, creating Web sites and learning how to surf and to navigate skillfully.

Databases and electronic dictionaries can be used as a research tool when searching for definitions of historical language influences, or as background material for creative writing. A class might create their own databases on various backgrounds and structures to provide a resource of personal views, comments and related work undertaken by pupils.

There are also programs which simulate a busy newsroom with reports coming in through teletext, requiring the reading, selecting, condensing and representing of information from reports sent in by reporters that need to be converted into radio or front page news.

Class E-mail and inter-school links can be used to communicate with readers outside the classroom. Pupils can send 'published' work, or drafts of work in progress, to be edited by another class.

Transforming texts – manipulating form and changing text

Pupils can use the computer to change a narrative into a script, focusing on form, structure, syntax, punctuation and presentation. They can select elements from a CD-ROM to use in a newspaper report, story, poem, poster, argument/debate.

Texts can be condensed and expanded to investigate figures of speech, aspects of genre, style, language and presentation. Pupils can experiment with a richer use of adverbs and adjectives, altering the gender of a narrative, re-jigging the nouns to alter narrative style and tone, offering different endings, characters, and for other features of editing.

Assessing speaking and listening

A specific area of concern for teachers of English is the question of the assessment of speaking and listening in lessons that are ICT-based. These can be group-work lessons and can be assessed as such, or the main channel of the lesson's work that is discussed as a whole class at the end of the lesson. Essentially, pupils will respond to ICT texts and work as they will to any other stimulus: through talk.

Further Information

The benefits of using ICT in subject teaching
Objectives in the use of ICT
Literacy and ICT
SEN and ICT
Assessing the use of ICT
Flexible learning resources
Using word processing software
Using multimedia software
Communicating information

Standards

2

Trainees must be taught how to use ICT most effectively in relation to subject-related objectives, including:

a. using ICT because it is the most effective way to achieve teaching and learning objectives, not simply to motivate pupils or as a reward or sanction for good or poor work or behaviour;

b. avoiding the use of ICT for simple or routine tasks which would be better accomplished by other means;

c. knowing that, where ICT is to be used, appropriate preparation of equipment, content and methodology is required;

d. avoiding giving the impression that the quality of presentation is of overriding importance and supersedes the importance of content;

e. structuring pupils' work to focus on relevant aspects and to maximise use of time and resource;

f. having high expectations of the outcomes of pupils' work with ICT, including:

· expecting pupils to use ICT to answer valid questions appropriate to the subject matter being taught;

· when appropriate, requiring pupils to save work, and evaluate and improve it;

g. making explicit the links between:

   i the ICT application and the subject matter it is being used to teach;

   ii ICT and its impact on everyday applications.

17

Trainees must demonstrate that they know how each of the following is relevant to the specialist subject and phase for which they are training:

a. **generic procedures and tools,** including

   i. understanding the key features and functions used within the subject;

   ii. using ICT to prepare material for pupil use.

b. **reference resources,** including;

   i. how to search reference resources;

   ii. how to incorporate the use of reference resources into teaching.

c. **the ICT specific to the subject;**

d. **the major teaching programs or "courseware" to ensure that material is matched to the pupils' competences;**

ICT continues to have a large impact on how some areas of mathematics are taught in schools. The mathematics teacher can aid a pupil's understanding of mathematics with the use of ICT to achieve things which would be difficult and time-consuming using conventional methods.

In a review of software for the teaching of mathematics BECTa identified the following types of software in use in mathematics teaching:

- small software programs aimed at highly specific content, e.g. place value, histograms or vectors
- programming languages, e.g. *Logo*, Prolog
- generic software, e.g. spreadsheets and databases
- content-free, subject specific, e.g. graph plotting, computer algebra (CAS), and dynamic geometry software (DGS)
- courseware: structured materials with integral software, e.g. ILS
- graphical calculators
- CD-ROMs and the Internet.

The publication *Mathematics and IT: a pupil's entitlement*, from BECTa / CITS, categorised the use of the software outlined above to deliver the mathematics curriculum under six categories.

Learning from feedback

Well-established practice with tools such as *Logo* used to create visual patterns gives the pupils the opportunity to learn while appearing to 'play'. The re-inforcement of basic number skills that pupils learn in primary school is always important. Classroom practice, games and activities are a good way of achieving this and ICT can play an important role. ICT gives the opportunity to practise and re-inforce skills and ideas. There are a large number of inexpensive, small software tools focused on specific aspects of numeracy, e.g. *Smile*. These can be used to give support as part of teachers' differentiation strategies. Integrated learning systems are, of course, a very sophisticated diagnostic tool which exploit learning from feedback.

Observing patterns

Exploring number grids and patterns can now be achieved with spreadsheet software and calculators and can be extended, if CAS is available, into searching for algebraic patterns.

Seeing connections

Spreadsheets and graphical calculators allow pupils to handle tables of numeric data and link them to graphical outputs. The visual representation and instant feedback help pupils to understand the connection between them.

Working with dynamic images

When teaching circle theorems, pupils would traditionally draw out numerous circles and try to find out the relationships. Alternatively, they are told the theorems as facts

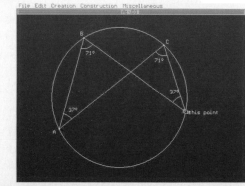

and then practise using them. There are a number of geometry software packages such as *Cabri Geometré*, that cannot only be used to demonstrate geometrical facts but can be used by pupils to investigate and discover rules for themselves. Diagrams are easily constructed and then manipulated. Angles and measurements are updated on the screen instantly, allowing students to observe which properties change and which do not. Pupils make notes of any observations and later can feed back their findings to the class.

Exploring data

Interpreting and analysing real data can be very motivating. Data can be obtained from the Internet, CD-ROM and, more recently, sensing equipment which can link directly to graphical calculators. Pupils engage in mathematical modelling as they decide how best to represent the data.

Teaching the computer

Using *Logo*, macro features in spreadsheets, DGS and the programming language of graphical calculators allows students to design algorithms (sets of instructions) to make the computer perform specific operations. Programming is still alive and well!

Coursework

The use of software such as spreadsheets, CAD, MathCAD and graph plotters, such as *Omnigraph* can be used to enhance pupils' work and allows them to present their findings in a professional way.

When to use IT

- Investigate number patterns in spreadsheets, e.g. triangle numbers, square numbers, the Fibonacci series, Pascal's triangle.
- Use the Internet to find out more about mathematical ideas, e.g. Fibonacci series.
- Investigate straight line graphs, move onto to investigate parabolas.
- Most investigations can be produced using a spreadsheet and the spreadsheet can be used to check equations.
- Carry out surveys, enter the results into a database, analyse the results, produce graphs. Investigate suitable graphs for displaying the data.
- Compare results and assess whether data/results are accurate.

When not to use IT

- When certain skills, such as graph plotting, are the main learning objective.
- If demonstration of a method needs to be taught to everyone.

Exploring data: the container problem

'A favourite coursework problem is to design a container to hold a product, e.g. stock cubes or, for the more able, perhaps a salt container.

Pupils can look at cuboids, pyramids, cones and many other solids. Formulas for volume and surface area can be created. Then a trial and improvement approach can be used to find solutions.

To minimise surface area while maintaining a required volume can be achieved by traditional methods, but pupils who have access to spreadsheets can model the problem and find solutions to any level of accuracy.

Repetitive number searching is avoided. Graphs can be created so that a minimum can be physically identified. CAD software can be used to create nets for these solids.'

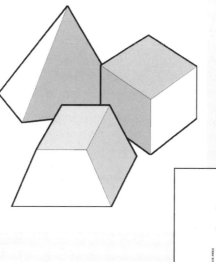

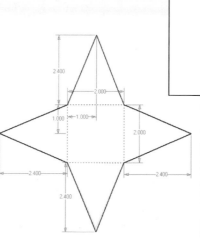

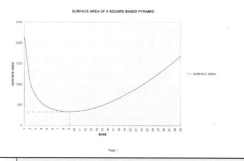

Further Information

The benefits of ICT in subject teaching
Objectives in the use of ICT
Assessing the use of ICT
Flexible learning resources
Using spreadsheet software
Automatic functions (1): control
Trying things out: modelling

Standards

2

Trainees must be taught how to use ICT most effectively in relation to subject-related objectives, including:

a. using ICT because it is the most effective way to achieve teaching and learning objectives, not simply to motivate pupils or as a reward or sanction for good or poor work or behaviour;

b. avoiding the use of ICT for simple or routine tasks which would be better accomplished by other means;

c. knowing that, where ICT is to be used, appropriate preparation of equipment, content and methodology is required;

d. avoiding giving the impression that the quality of presentation is of overriding importance and supersedes the importance of content;

e. structuring pupils' work to focus on relevant aspects and to maximise use of time and resource;

f. having high expectations of the outcomes of pupils' work with ICT, including:

· expecting pupils to use ICT to answer valid questions appropriate to the subject matter being taught;

· when appropriate, requiring pupils to save work, and evaluate and improve it;

g. making explicit the links between:

　i　the ICT application and the subject matter it is being used to teach;

　ii　ICT and its impact on everyday applications.

17

Trainees must demonstrate that they know how each of the following is relevant to the specialist subject and phase for which they are training:

a. **generic procedures and tools,** including
　i. understanding the key features and functions used within the subject;
　ii. using ICT to prepare material for pupil use.

b. **reference resources,** including;
　i. how to search reference resources;
　ii. how to incorporate the use of reference resources into teaching.

c. **the ICT specific to the subject;**

d. the major teaching programs or "courseware" to ensure that material is matched to the pupils' ompetences;

Teachers of Science have been some of the earliest proponents for the effectiveness of ICT to inform, motivate and explore. Most aspects of ICT can enhance teaching and learning in Science: a considerable challenge for Science teachers!

Scientists use ICT tools as part of their work to:

- collect information automatically
- handle data from experiments
- model ideas
- search for information
- present information and data.

In classrooms teachers will want to work in ways that illustrate how scientists exploit the power of ICT.

Collecting data from experiments

Electronic sensing equipment can assist in the capture of experimental results. The technology is not an alternative to learning how to measure variables with conventional instruments but it can make it possible to record data that is difficult and/or expensive. It is most effective where it allows teachers and pupils to record data from experiments where the phenomena happen very slowly, very quickly or are generally hard to measure, for example: the growth of a plant; the extension of a paper tissue; or the acceleration of an object due to gravity.

Datalogging software not only collects but also organises the data in tables, graphs and charts that enable pupils to evaluate the results quickly and to decide if another run of the experiment is required. The easy collection of data motivates pupils to be more scientific in their experimental technique. Running the experiment again and again allows pupils to see experimental error and to test variables over a greater range of values.

Handling data from experiments

One of the core skills in handling experimental results in the classroom is the ability of the pupils to present and graph data in an informative way. This is often called graphical capability or graphicacy. Spreadsheets, in particular, can offer access and support in presenting and interpreting experimental data for a wide range of pupil capability:

- they take the pain out of graph plotting
- they adjust scales to suit the data
- they can graph accurately
- pupils can quickly view different types of graph and evaluate their effectiveness.

Modelling ideas

Computer models are an important feature of scientific activity to which pupils should be introduced. Pupils will need to be introduced to simple models, which they test by changing a variable to see the effects on dependent variables. At a later stage they can be taught to construct their own simple models.

Investigating the impact of changing variables in a simulation of a phenomenon which is too fast or too slow to investigate in the school laboratory. Explore the behaviour of a model by asking 'What if...' questions. For example, see the effect of withdrawing particular foods from the model of a balanced diet. Simulations are a subset of modelling activity. Pupils can investigate the effect of changing variables in a system or process which would be difficult, dangerous or take too long. For example, as manager of a wild-life reserve the user can see the ecological consequences of certain decisions.

Searching for information

Teaching for, or using databases, is one of the more difficult aspects of IT in Science. Compiling and creating school databases can be undertaken as a class activity but this is time-consuming and needs organisation. Commercial data sets can be purchased to provide data files associated with particular areas of the curriculum. These can provide large quantities of data which would be difficult to create in a school environment. Some require specific software but more recently publishers are tending to supply data for generic Windows packages such as *Access* and *Excel*.

The popularity of CD-ROM databases has opened up access to large quantities of data without the learning curve often involved in creating a database from scratch. The ease of access to images and data can be very motivating when pupils are researching secondary sources.

The Internet can offer pupils the opportunity to:

- search on-line data bases for information on chemical hazards
- talk to scientists via chat pages
- visit museums and research facilities around the world
- follow the progress of a space mission
- communicate/share results of investigations between schools.

Presentation of results and ideas

Word processors and DTP offer Science teachers a number of different opportunities to develop pupils' basic skills in the presentation of information. Teachers often offer a chain of instructions to pupils for practical work, which are rarely internalised. Actively thinking through a sequence can imprint it deeper on the understanding. Pupils, working in pairs, can use the 'drag and drop' feature of *Word* to organise the sequence of events within an experiment. This saves time on copying and allows time for thinking and discussion.

Pupils can use DTP:

- to present their research findings to peers
- as an assessable outcome of scientific enquiry
- as a vehicle for extracting/organising information related to text (DARTS)
- to gather a variety of data: spreadsheets, graphs, pictures, text and organise into a coherent presentation. For example, can renewable energy sources provide an alternative to nuclear power?
- to summarise an investigation pupils could draw together descriptions of the process of the investigation, data in the form of tables and graphs, and graphic diagrams.

When not to use IT

It is important, whenever possible, that ICT activities are not undertaken in isolation but are an integral part of scientific activity. The computer in the corner of the laboratory enables pupils to exploit the potential of ICT for capturing and handling data or searching for information as a natural part of scientific investigations.

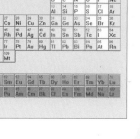

Further Information

The benefits of ICT in subject teaching
Objectives in the use of ICT
Numeracy and ICT
Assessing the use of ICT
Using spreadsheet software
Automatic functions (2): sensing
Trying things out: modelling
Using ICT to find things out

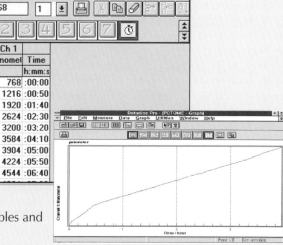

Teaching with ICT

Standards

2

Trainees must be taught how to use ICT most effectively in relation to subject-related objectives, including:

a. using ICT because it is the most effective way to achieve teaching and learning objectives, not simply to motivate pupils or as a reward or sanction for good or poor work or behaviour;

b. avoiding the use of ICT for simple or routine tasks which would be better accomplished by other means;

c. knowing that, where ICT is to be used, appropriate preparation of equipment, content and methodology is required;

d. avoiding giving the impression that the quality of presentation is of overriding importance and supersedes the importance of content;

e. structuring pupils' work to focus on relevant aspects and to maximise use of time and resource;

f. having high expectations of the outcomes of pupils' work with ICT, including:

  · expecting pupils to use ICT to answer valid questions appropriate to the subject matter being taught;

  · when appropriate, requiring pupils to save work, and evaluate and improve it;

g. making explicit the links between:

  i the ICT application and the subject matter it is being used to teach;

  ii ICT and its impact on everyday applications.

17

Trainees must demonstrate that they know how each of the following is relevant to the specialist subject and phase for which they are training:

a. generic procedures and tools, including

  i. understanding the key features and functions used within the subject;

  ii. using ICT to prepare material for pupil use.

b. reference resources, including;

  i. how to search reference resources;

  ii. how to incorporate the use of reference resources into teaching.

c. the ICT specific to the subject;

d. the major teaching programs or "courseware" to ensure that material is matched to the pupils' competences;

Design and Technology provides an unusual opportunity for pupils to use the full range of ICT to design and make products. In particular, CAD-CAM systems enhance the processes of developing ideas and of understanding control in manufacturing.

Drawing and DTP packages

2D and 3D drawing packages enable pupils to generate, explore and communicate ideas rapidly and easily. Graphic and DTP packages can be used to combine text with graphics in the design of packaging, leaflets, posters, etc. Programs such as *Crocodile Clips* enable pupils to experiment with electronic circuits and simple mechanical systems. CAD packages permit the development of 3D forms.

The basic tools of professional 2D packages can be mastered easily by most pupils, and some will be capable of producing sophisticated results. Although these programs are becoming easier to use, many younger pupils will find 3D CAD packages initially inhibiting. Pupils should be taught how professional designers use CAD systems in an industrial context.

It is important not to let pupils use CAD exclusively during the development of design ideas. At times the transformation tools the computer provides suggest new directions and possibilities that would not have been generated simply using pencil and paper, but a cavalcade of pre-set electronic special effects is often offered as a substitute for fine judgements about the purpose of and audience for the design. Developing ideas should involve a mixture of annotated sketching, computer experimentation, external evaluation of print-outs, card modelling, etc.

Computer-aided manufacture (CAM)

Computer files created on a CAD system can be used directly to produce accurate, high quality manufactured products. Usually this will be undertaken in the school, using computer-controlled sewing or knitting machines, milling machines, lathes, cutter-plotters, engraving machines, etc. Where suitable facilities exist the data can alternatively be transmitted directly to a remote site where perhaps more sophisticated manufacturing equipment is available.

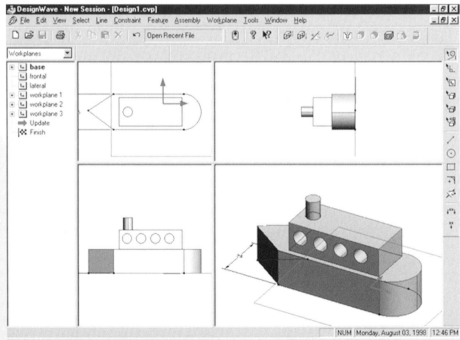

DesignWave from Parametric Technology Corporation

Databases

Searching for relevant information is an important design skill which can be enhanced through ICT. Pupils might find information about materials and components, anthropometric data, nutritional values, visual images, etc., either from databases compiled in school or obtained from CD-ROMs and the Internet.

Spreadsheets

One popular use of spreadsheets in Design and Technology is to enter data which can then be presented visually in the form of graphs or charts for analysis. In other situations spreadsheets can be used effectively for costing design alterations, e.g. predicting the impact on the cost of changing a particular component when different quantities are to be produced.

Control systems

Computers can be used to control sequences of events (e.g. traffic lights) and respond to external heat, light and motion sensors.

Further Information

The benefits of ICT in subject teaching
Objectives in the use of ICT
Assessing the use of ICT
Using spreadsheet software
Using database software
Using graphics software
Automatic functions (1): control
Trying things out: modelling

Blocking out the sun....

'I wanted to introduce my Year 7 pupils to a simple CAD package and a paint package, alongside giving them some experience in working in wood and with fabric.

The project began by evaluating the quality of the workshop environment. The task was then focused on to the window blinds, which were a plain cream colour.

The pupils were shown how to use a CAD program to select, combine and experiment with an arrangement of geometric shapes. These would form the basis of a block design which would be printed onto the blinds. Their final designs were printed out and used as a template to cut out their patterns in relief from a 10cm square block of wood.

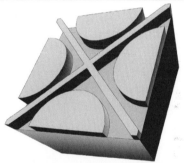

The pupils imported their designs from the CAD program into a paint program. Here they were able to experiment with different colour combinations. They were also able to copy and paste the block motif in different positions to explore the most effective pattern repeat for the finished blinds. They were often surprised by the difference that changing just one colour or the position of each block print made. To work through so many possibilities would have taken ages.

Finally they used their blocks to print up a series of fabric samples.'

(Based on a case study published in *Getting IT Across*, NCET, 1993)

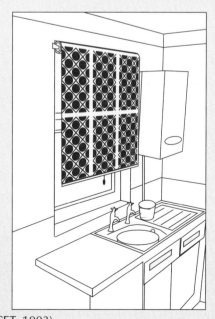

Standards

2

Trainees must be taught how to use ICT most effectively in relation to subject-related objectives, including:

a. using ICT because it is the most effective way to achieve teaching and learning objectives, not simply to motivate pupils or as a reward or sanction for good or poor work or behaviour;

b. avoiding the use of ICT for simple or routine tasks which would be better accomplished by other means;

c. knowing that, where ICT is to be used, appropriate preparation of equipment, content and methodology is required;

d. avoiding giving the impression that the quality of presentation is of overriding importance and supersedes the importance of content;

e. structuring pupils' work to focus on relevant aspects and to maximise use of time and resource;

f. having high expectations of the outcomes of pupils' work with ICT, including:
   - expecting pupils to use ICT to answer valid questions appropriate to the subject matter being taught;
   - when appropriate, requiring pupils to save work, and evaluate and improve it;

g. making explicit the links between:
   i   the ICT application and the subject matter it is being used to teach;
   ii ICT and its impact on everyday applications.

17

Trainees must demonstrate that they know how each of the following is relevant to the specialist subject and phase for which they are training:

a. generic procedures and tools, including
   i   understanding the key features and functions used within the subject;
   ii using ICT to prepare material for pupil use.

b. reference resources, including;
   i   how to search reference resources;
   ii how to incorporate the use of reference resources into teaching.

c. the ICT specific to the subject;

d. the major teaching programs or "courseware" to ensure that material is matched to the pupils' competences;

There is a vast amount of material available for use in the Geography classroom, both on CD-ROM and the Internet, as well as other software packages which offer interactive learning.

ICT provides pupils with access to people and places that they may not otherwise reach. Geography can sometimes be an abstract and 'far-away' subject and some of the ICT applications below can help pupils link the class lessons to real situations and real people and thus give the subject more credence in the pupils' minds. It also provides the opportunity for geographical enquiry that is not restricted to pencil and paper activity.

ICT in Geography can:

- enhance geographical enquiry skills
- allow access to a wide range of geographical knowledge and information
- aid the student's spatial and environmental relationship
- develop knowledge of an alternative lifestyle or culture
- help pupils consider the wider impact of IT on people, places and the environment.

Databases, spreadsheets and subject specific software packages are amongst the most commonly used forms of IT employed in Geography classrooms.

Spreadsheets and databases

Spreadsheets and databases enable analytical work to be carried out on data and encourage pupils to look for patterns and relationships as well as interpret and decipher data collected in investigations from automatic weather and data logging software. A set of readings from beach, cliff or river channel profiles can be manipulated into an impressive 3D graph which is then imported into a word processing package.

Quality of life indicators (e.g. public safety – murders per 100,000 people; living space – persons per room) for the metropolitan areas and counties can be stored in a spreadsheet form. This can be manipulated later by a class, by ranking the areas in ascending or descending order and presenting the results in a variety of graphs (pie charts, block, line, scatter-graphs, etc.)

A database can be constructed by the class from local and national weather observations (available by fax or from the Internet). This can be used to study weather patterns. Importing the data into a spreadsheet can produce graphs in order to prove that there are urban heat islands.

Databases can be used to store information from questionnaires and results using queries can then be exported. This is especially useful for Year 11 and Year 13 projects.

Many schools are using satellite receiving and analysis equipment and accessing the Internet. Both word processing and desktop publishing software are used especially for individual projects or for displays and presentations. The Internet offers a world of opportunity for real activities and for collecting information from around the world. There is also an increasing variety of software packages for subject-specific activities.

'I asked a group of pupils to use a CD-ROM and the Internet as part of their investigation about the Mississippi Flood. I prepared a worksheet which asked them to identify various pieces of evidence to show that the flood caused serious damage to property and the economy.

They were also asked to use the information they discovered to reach a conclusion about a more open-ended question about human intervention along the Mississippi, making the effects of flooding more serious.'

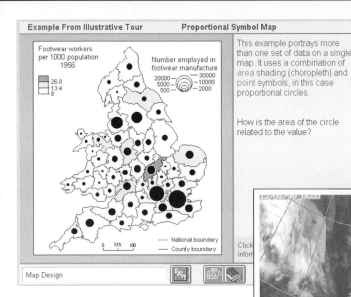

When to use ICT
- When ICT allows pupils to: manipulate, interpret, predict and display information (including fieldwork), pose questions, test hypotheses, analyse and evaluate information.

When not to use ICT
- When there is a risk of over-using the computer as a tool and a resource as well as students plagiarising other people's work.
- Students should have the opportunity to use 'real' maps, create 'real' graphs, etc. and not to rely on 'virtual' tools.

Word processors and desk top publishing packages
A class could use word processors to record the findings of their enquiry of a local industry as well as checking their grammar and spelling. The pupils' knowledge of another lifestyle or culture can then be printed and displayed in the classroom. Data from the Internet, spreadsheet graphs, clip art, scanned diagrams and photographs can be added to the text. A class can be set a task to find relevant information about a country or area that they have studied and present it using the DTP package. ICT can also be used to create questionnaires, time and data sheets in preparation of a project.

Internet and electronic mail
The Internet is best used to search for current data, whether this is a satellite image of a recent volcanic plume, the strength and exact location of an earthquake, the protection for the British coasts, the variations in farming types in Britain, or the percentages of primary, secondary and tertiary industries of various countries to discover their development. The World Wide Web can do all this and more. The Internet could also be used to create a Geography-related Web site with examples of class work.

Teachers could create a link with another Geography department in another county or country and communicate using E-mail as well as sending examples of class work to save time on lesson preparation. One department had contact with a Japanese school before and after the Kobe earthquake!

Multimedia
CD-ROMs can include 'virtual' models which are hard to create in a classroom; DK *Earthquest* has a volcanic eruption and an earthquake which react to the parameters chosen. Maps of varying types and magnifications can be used to enhance the pupil's spatial relationship or classroom discussions. Ordnance Survey have superb digital maps which are available over the Internet. Sophisticated independent-learning packages such as *Geography Calc* illustrate the potential of the resource for examination courses.

Sensing
Relatively accurate local weather data can be collected using a purpose-built electronic weather station or using datalogging equipment and a variety of sensors (e.g. pressure, temperature, light). This data can be displayed using the proprietary software or exported to a spreadsheet.

Further Information:

Standards

2

Trainees must be taught how to use ICT most effectively in relation to subject-related objectives, including:

a. using ICT because it is the most effective way to achieve teaching and learning objectives, not simply to motivate pupils or as a reward or sanction for good or poor work or behaviour;

b. avoiding the use of ICT for simple or routine tasks which would be better accomplished by other means;

c. knowing that, where ICT is to be used, appropriate preparation of equipment, content and methodology is required;

d. avoiding giving the impression that the quality of presentation is of overriding importance and supersedes the importance of content;

e. structuring pupils' work to focus on relevant aspects and to maximise use of time and resource;

f. having high expectations of the outcomes of pupils' work with ICT, including:
   - expecting pupils to use ICT to answer valid questions appropriate to the subject matter being taught;
   - when appropriate, requiring pupils to save work, and evaluate and improve it;

g. making explicit the links between:
   i   the ICT application and the subject matter it is being used to teach;
   ii ICT and its impact on everyday applications.

17

Trainees must demonstrate that they know how each of the following is relevant to the specialist subject and phase for which they are training:

a. **generic procedures and tools**, including
   i   understanding the key features and functions used within the subject;
   ii using ICT to prepare material for pupil use.

b. **reference resources**, including;
   i   how to search reference resources;
   ii how to incorporate the use of reference resources into teaching.

c. **the ICT specific to the subject;**

d. the major teaching programs or "courseware" to ensure that material is matched to the pupils' competences;

The computer offers the historian powerful tools for investigation, research analysis and presentation of findings. Data handling software, simulations and data sources such as CD-ROM and the Internet now supplement video and audio materials.

In History ICT can:
- support investigation and research of written and pictorial sources;
- develop historical understanding through simulation packages;
- aid in the collation and presentation of historical findings using word processed format, spreadsheets, databases, or presentation packages (e.g. *PowerPoint*) for the communication of findings to an audience.

Searching for information

The Internet can provide unusual material, perspectives and interpretations. CD-ROMs specifically aimed at History provide a wealth of focused data on particular periods. Pupils need to be clear that they are searching for information to address an historical issue. Resource banks of images or full-text databases of newspapers provide huge storehouses of information: too much information can present as much of a problem as too little. Pupils will require a plan, objectives and a strategy that will enable them to search effectively.

On CD-ROM and the Internet, in addition to searching by browsing a list of resources, there may be a time-line, a search by type (i.e. picture, video, text, etc.), a key word search or hypertext listings. Internet search engines, like *Altavista*, and many CD-ROMs allow key word searches. On the Internet there may be millions of references to a key word search, e.g. 'Second World War'. Refining the search is a key skill that pupils will need to be taught. Interested parties and organisations have also created pages of hypertext links to the best resources, e.g. the *Directory of History Resources*, maintains hundreds of 'pointers' that automatically connect with historical sites all over the world. It is organised alphabetically, by era and by subject.

When to use IT?

ICT is effectively used when it:

- helps pupils organise and communicate ideas more effectively;
- is an efficient and enhancing way of accessing information and evidence;
- develops skills, knowledge and understanding through the Key Elements of the National Curriculum;
- is part of a lesson/task which has a clear focus.

When not to use IT

- When the lesson is merely a chance to 'spice up' the presentation of a history essay.
- When care has not been taken to select and focus the pupils' attention on extracts and 'bite-size' chunks of evidence of a suitable length and/or complexity.
- An IT lesson will be wasting the teacher's and the pupils' time if some investigative objectives and historical issues have not been made clear beforehand.

Questions on purpose of activity

- What will be the end product from a computer session?
- Will you be able to assess the work?
- Does it provide continuity and progression in your Scheme of Work?
- Does it relate to a Key Element, e.g. Historical Enquiry or Organisation and Communication?
- Have the pupils shown progression in the development of IT skills?

Using a word processor

Using a generic program such as a word processor, can enhance the quality of learning in History. Text-based evidence can be interrogated, analysed and organised. Word processors are often described as 'thought processors'! Writing frames containing prompts, created by the teacher, can structure pupils' writing.

Creating and using Data files

Data files can help pupils to search for patterns in past events and identify regional or national trends. A modest data file provided as a spreadsheet file can become the source material for an historical enquiry.

Was the experience of war for civilians the same in Britain, France and Germany?

Pupils at Key Stage 3 use a text-based archive provided as word processor files. The texts are transcripts of interviews, reminiscences and monologues from the three countries. Pupils undertake a series of guided searches through the files, using lists of key words provided by the teacher. The information is entered into a table where headings suggest ways of organising finding. Pupils complete their report using a 'writing frame' template that suggests a structure to present the evidence.

Why did the Roman Empire fail?

Key Stage 3 pupils used data provided as spreadsheet files to answer a succession of questions. The data contained on the files offered information on the Roman Emperors and the campaigns they fought.

What happened to the Emperors?

Where did the Emperors come from?

What were the threats to the Empire?

Pupils went on to create a small database of their own using data from books and a CD-ROM. The different types of source were categorised in a table and informed pupils' choice of fields within the database. Finally pupils used the database to answer some key questions:

What information is plentiful about the Romans?

What aspects of the Roman Empire is there less information on?

Further information

The benefits of ICT in subject teaching
Objectives in the use of ICT
Assessing the use of ICT
Using database software
Using multimedia software
Using the Internet
Using ICT to find things out

Standards

2

Trainees must be taught how to use ICT most effectively in relation to subject-related objectives, including:

a. using ICT because it is the most effective way to achieve teaching and learning objectives, not simply to motivate pupils or as a reward or sanction for good or poor work or behaviour;

b. avoiding the use of ICT for simple or routine tasks which would be better accomplished by other means;

c. knowing that, where ICT is to be used, appropriate preparation of equipment, content and methodology is required;

d. avoiding giving the impression that the quality of presentation is of overriding importance and supersedes the importance of content;

e. structuring pupils' work to focus on relevant aspects and to maximise use of time and resource;

f. having high expectations of the outcomes of pupils' work with ICT, including:

   • expecting pupils to use ICT to answer valid questions appropriate to the subject matter being taught;

   • when appropriate, requiring pupils to save work, and evaluate and improve it;

g. making explicit the links between:

   i   the ICT application and the subject matter it is being used to teach;

   ii ICT and its impact on everyday applications.

17

Trainees must demonstrate that they know how each of the following is relevant to the specialist subject and phase for which they are training:

a. **generic procedures and tools**, including

   i. understanding the key features and functions used within the subject;

   ii. using ICT to prepare material for pupil use.

b. **reference resources,** including;

   i. how to search reference resources;

   ii. how to incorporate the use of reference resources into teaching.

c. **the ICT specific to the subject;**

d. the major teaching programs or "courseware" to ensure that material is matched to the pupils' competences;

Computers offer the opportunity to:

• *improve language writing skills*

• *access authentic materials*

• *establish the conceptual links between languages*

• *provide active and exciting opportunities to practise and drill language forms.*

Foreign language learning is enhanced by direct and authentic contact with foreign speakers and foreign cultures through the use of ICT.

Improving communication

A variety of applications can be used to meet the subject objectives.

Word processing

Developing the skill of writing in a foreign language requires purpose and direction. Using the word processor allows learners to generate texts of interest and of professional quality. Producing brochures, recipes, menus, phrase books, and incorporating pictures means that pupils can contribute in a more meaningful way. Correcting work on the screen enriches the process of drafting and re-drafting, providing an opportunity for research and enquiry work to be presented in a more professional manner. Formal letter writing is authenticated by formal presentation. Cutting and pasting, the use of different font sizes and styles all contribute to meaning, and the development of appropriate paralinguistic skills gives the learner the opportunity to participate, whatever their ability in the foreign language.

Databases

The collection of data and information through realistic and authentic foreign language can be presented in a meaningful, structured manner. Classroom surveys and paper-based research in the target language can be recorded and presented professionally, and themes and topics can be updated as they are revisited throughout the curriculum. For personal use learners can categorise vocabulary and phrases, thereby enhancing their own study skills and learning strategies.

Internet and E-mail

The Internet provides almost limitless support for the classroom researcher. The immediate provision of authentic materials, as well as a growing number of language learning games, relieves the teacher of the responsibility to search continuously for real examples of texts. Through E-mail links with Internet users abroad, learners have an authentic audience for their work. Enthusiastic correspondents can provide immediate feedback to questionnaires, enquiries and through on-line electronic conferences.

'My Year 9 pupils investigate a holiday town in France. They use authentic resources on other holiday areas that have been collected by the teacher and previous pupils. On the Internet they locate the region and the town and download information in French as a text file, saving the images separately. Enquiries are made of the tourist information service by E-mail and fax.

The pupils work in groups, using Microsoft Publisher to assemble their guide aimed at a French language audience visiting the town.'

When to use IT

- To support independent language learning.
- To communicate in the target language.
- To access a range of resources in the target language and identify with the people.
- To meet any special needs for access to language learning.

When not to use IT

- There is a risk of over-use of American English.
- Computers are not the language laboratories of the 21st Century .
- Computers should support, not replace, interpersonal communication.

Multimedia

CD-ROMs can provide the opportunity for learners to practise and develop competence in the skills of reading, writing, listening and speaking within an interactive context. Learners can participate in on-screen dialogues, engage in drill exercises and respond to written and heard stimuli with visual and contextual support. CD-ROMs designed to support published courses, to relate to communicative themes and/or to support grammatical learning, all provide endless opportunities for independent study and differentiation.

CD-ROM reference materials, such as back issues of newspapers, foreign versions of encyclopedias, dictionaries and thesauruses inevitably enhance the possibility for target language research.

Multimedia authoring packages

Packages are available which allow teachers and learners who have no knowledge of programming computers to create exercises following a given framework. As a means of devising support materials, and revision programmes the packages provide a further opportunity to support independent learning. Learners are able to devise images, manipulate and experiment with techniques alongside more traditional methods.

Concept keyboard

The danger of word-for-word translation can be overcome by use of the concept keyboard. Keyboard pads designated to represent words, phrases and even sentences facilitate the development of scripts for dialogues by removing the inhibitive stress of accuracy. The concept keyboard provides the detail in terms of spelling, allowing learners to focus on meaning, yet to have correct versions reinforced through the written word. Word processing the outcomes allows for editing and the personalisation of established concepts.

Further Information

The benefits of ICT in subject teaching
Objectives in the use of ICT
Assessing the use of ICT
Flexible learning resources
Using word processing software
Using multimedia software
Communicating information
Using database software
Using ICT to find things out

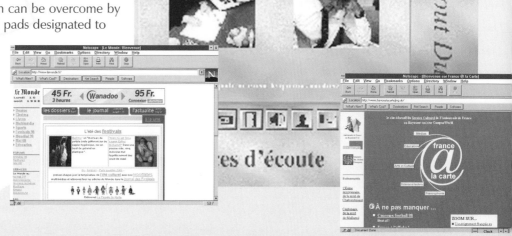

Standards

2

Trainees must be taught how to use ICT most effectively in relation to subject-related objectives, including:

a. using ICT because it is the most effective way to achieve teaching and learning objectives, not simply to motivate pupils or as a reward or sanction for good or poor work or behaviour;

b. avoiding the use of ICT for simple or routine tasks which would be better accomplished by other means;

c. knowing that, where ICT is to be used, appropriate preparation of equipment, content and methodology is required;

d. avoiding giving the impression that the quality of presentation is of overriding importance and supersedes the importance of content;

e. structuring pupils' work to focus on relevant aspects and to maximise use of time and resource;

f. having high expectations of the outcomes of pupils' work with ICT, including:
   • expecting pupils to use ICT to answer valid questions appropriate to the subject matter being taught;
   • when appropriate, requiring pupils to save work, and evaluate and improve it;

g. making explicit the links between:
   i   the ICT application and the subject matter it is being used to teach;
   ii ICT and its impact on everyday applications.

17

Trainees must demonstrate that they know how each of the following is relevant to the specialist subject and phase for which they are training:

a. generic procedures and tools, including
   i. understanding the key features and functions used within the subject;
   ii. using ICT to prepare material for pupil use.

b. reference resources, including;
   i. how to search reference resources;
   ii. how to incorporate the use of reference resources into teaching.

c. the ICT specific to the subject;

d. the major teaching programs or "courseware" to ensure that material is matched to the pupils' competences;

Sophisticated image manipulation software is now available at a price that schools can afford. Pupils can now use computers to create, experiment with and produce final pieces of art and design work. Other packages can be used to support work in critical studies.

Origination

There are several ways of establishing images on a computer in a digital format. The main sources are:

• drawn images produced by the pupil using a computer drawing package and either a mouse or drawing tablet (alternatively, original drawings or other images produced by the pupil can be scanned in)

• external images gained from scanning or digital photography

• existing images that already exist as digital information, such as photographs or clipart taken from a CD-ROM, or downloaded from a Web site.

Scanning enables pupils to experiment with 2D and 3D source materials. Artists who have worked with photocopiers, printing techniques and or photography illustrate the possibilities.

Composing and manipulating

Once on-screen there are a wide variety of ways in which images can be composed and transformed. Colours, shapes and textures can be altered, text can be added and/or a photo-manipulation package used to experiment with various distortions and overlays.

Tasks which are simple to perform on the computer can quickly appear complicated and sophisticated, with a minimum of effort or consideration. For example, in the production of a poster or leaflet a combination of fonts, graphic shapes and colours and clip art could easily result in a predictable and uninteresting design. However, if elements of the image are combined with a scanner, photocopier or collage, or printed over painted washes or textured backgrounds, then the project can be transformed into something much more expressive, considered and exciting.

Production

The form of the final image can be viewed in one of two formats:

• *Digital format*: the piece may best be represented on the computer screen itself, e.g. as an animated moving image or a Web site page.

• *Hard copy*: work can be printed out in colour or black-and-white. Just as the printed photograph can be enhanced during printing, so the computer image can be enhanced by experimentation at the production stage. If an image is printed onto a surface that does not absorb the ink, e.g. foil, it can then be transferred by rubbing onto another surface or, as most inks are water-based, the image could be manipulated further with brush and water.

Critical studies

There are many ways of linking Art history work areas with ICT. The Internet and CD-ROM resources provide a rich source of information on artists, movements and theories, drawn from libraries, museums and galleries across the world. Many artists explored the technology of their time, from Piero della Francesca to Warhol, presenting challenging and exciting new works and concepts. The techniques used in movements such as Pop Art, Cubism, Fauvism, Impressionism and Modernism lend themselves well to processes of on-screen image manipulation.

Integrating ICT into existing projects

While some activities might be led by the use of ICT, in most cases teachers need to look at existing projects to identify opportunities for using computers as a tool.

'I run a project with my Year 8 group to design a stamp with a multicultural theme. Pupils begin by finding out how other cultures represent themselves through artefacts. As well as the usual sources of information such as books and magazines, I decided to suggest exploring the Internet. This quickly produced a range of new and exciting images and gave the pupils a broader view of the particular culture they were investigating.

Using this material the pupils then produced a series of paintings, mixed media, 3D works, etc. with the intention of forming the basis of a design for a stamp, illustrating the culture explored. I began to encourage pupils to scan their work into the computer and use a graphics package to refine the design and to add text and a profile of the Queen's head. The final image can then be reduced and printed out in colour to produce an effective and realistic stamp design.'

When to use IT

When ICT allows pupils to:

- explore situations and visualise the outcomes of different approaches, methods and techniques
- access a wide variety of visual resources
- inform themselves of methods and techniques in historical and cultural contexts.

When not to use IT

- As the definitive means for producing the image. Experiment with other media and combine the results.
- Computers should support not replace interpersonal communication.

Questions for teachers

- Is there enough memory to save and process images?
- Does the task develop creative skills or just computing ability?
- Can the resources be managed to allow each pupil access?
- In what form is the final piece produced?
- How will works be saved or recorded?
- What outcomes will be used to assess pupils?
- How is the evidence of the stages in development to be presented and recorded?

Further Information

The benefits of ICT in subject teaching
Objectives in the use of ICT
Assessing the use of ICT
Using graphics software
Using multimedia software
Communicating information
Using ICT to find things out

Standards

2

Trainees must be taught how to use ICT most effectively in relation to subject-related objectives, including:

a. using ICT because it is the most effective way to achieve teaching and learning objectives, not simply to motivate pupils or as a reward or sanction for good or poor work or behaviour;

b. avoiding the use of ICT for simple or routine tasks which would be better accomplished by other means;

c. knowing that, where ICT is to be used, appropriate preparation of equipment, content and methodology is required;

d. avoiding giving the impression that the quality of presentation is of overriding importance and supersedes the importance of content;

e. structuring pupils' work to focus on relevant aspects and to maximise use of time and resource;

f. having high expectations of the outcomes of pupils' work with ICT, including:

- expecting pupils to use ICT to answer valid questions appropriate to the subject matter being taught;

- when appropriate, requiring pupils to save work, and evaluate and improve it;

g. making explicit the links between:

  i the ICT application and the subject matter it is being used to teach;

  ii ICT and its impact on everyday applications.

17

Trainees must demonstrate that they know how each of the following is relevant to the specialist subject and phase for which they are training:

a. **generic procedures and tools,** including

  i. understanding the key features and functions used within the subject;

  ii. using ICT to prepare material for pupil use.

b. **reference resources,** including;

  i. how to search reference resources;

  ii. how to incorporate the use of reference resources into teaching.

c. **the ICT specific to the subject;**

d. the major teaching programs or "courseware" to ensure that material is matched to the pupils' competences;

The term 'music technology' is usually applied to any situation where music or sound is subjected to electronic manipulation, including the use of simple hi-fi equipment and tape recorders.

A technological approach to Music can help pupils develop practical skills and musical understanding and can provide differentiated opportunities for all abilities.

Exploring, creating, performing and recording sounds

The advent of digital technology has enabled new and exciting opportunities in composing and performing through MIDI (Musical Instrument Digital Interface) as a means to interconnect electronic keyboards, synthesisers and effects processors, with powerful computer software (sequencers) to control them.

Recording and sound processing

The process of recording music (or amplifying a 'live' performance) provides pupils with opportunities to examine and electronically modify the sound produced. By using a mixing desk to equalise and balance strands of sound, a processor to add effects such as reverberation, and a synthesiser to create sounds, pupils will have a closer understanding of the nature of sounds and their construction. They will be better able to internalise and discriminate within and between the musical elements, particularly timbre and texture. Computers allow pupils to minutely analyse, merge and shape sounds by displaying a graphical representation of the various parameters of the sound.

MIDI sequencing

Music sequencing software (such as *Cubase*) when used with a sound card or synthesiser allows pupils to organise music and sounds into a composition, then save and play the result. The sequencer displays work graphically (enhancing understanding of structure) and can be used by pupils who are not instrumentalists and who cannot read conventional notation. The synthesiser and sequencer combination gives pupils unlimited opportunities to test and develop ideas and to experiment with and compare alternatives. It teaches them to listen to and evaluate their own work critically.

Music publishing

Most sequencers can also display and print work as musical notation. Some skill is needed to edit a score produced in this way into something that is a musically and stylistically coherent representation of the composition. It is all too easy to print something that looks professional but is musical nonsense!

Using MIDI in class

MIDI sequences can be used within a whole-class setting as listening exercises, or as backing tracks for the class orchestra. Their versatility means that tracks can be muted or transposed, tempi can be changed without affecting the pitch, and playback can be 'looped' as required. Sequences lend themselves to accompaniment in 'ceilidh' style, rehearsing parts freely without stopping.

Electronic keyboards

Electronic keyboards provide opportunities to investigate a range of sounds and styles. Pupils can explore instrumentation, tempo, pitch, rhythm patterns, and special effects. 'Single-finger' settings allow chords to be generated easily while a melody is improvised over the top. Simple melodic or chordal patterns can be sequenced into the memory.

Searching for, retrieving and processing information

CD-ROMs and the Internet provide dynamic new ways of accessing information relevant to Music. It is important that data is gathered selectively and with a clear objective, so that pupils do not merely print off entire articles but are able to collate, interpret and represent information in their own words.

CD-ROMs

The ability to store large amounts of information in the form of pictures, text and sound make CD-ROMs particularly suited for music topics. They can be encyclopedic (such as Microsoft's *Musical Instruments*, or *Encarta*), listening aids (a performance of a work with analytical notes, biographical detail and excerpts from the score), or instrumental tutors.

The Internet

The variety of ways the Internet can be used in a musical context include:

- researching textual and graphical information to develop pupils' musical and cultural knowledge
- increasing pupils' awareness of the commercial side of the music industry: artists, concerts, venues, recording and publishing companies, advertisements, career information
- downloading MIDI song files for evaluation and adaptation, (There are many examples freely available over the Internet covering all styles of music, variable in quality. Those demonstrating good technique can be models for pupils' own work.)
- downloading 'wave' files (short sound samples) for use in sequenced compositions
- obtaining information and advice concerning the use of music technology via news groups and discussion forums.
- E-mail allows rapid exchange of information with other classes or institutions. Compositions can be E-mailed in MIDI format for instant audition, or as music notation.

Using other software

Pupils can use databases and spreadsheets to maintain a log of compositions and performances together with evaluations. Commentaries to compositions can be word processed, especially where a printed score has been produced. Templates can be used to create a unified format when assembling a portfolio of work.

When to use ICT

When it allows pupils to:

- develop critical listening skills
- appraise and refine musical ideas
- use graphical tools to notate and display their composition work
- record and communicate musical ideas
- explore different styles of and from different periods and places
- perform compositions in different environments
- compose and control a range of sounds in the acoustic and electronic domain

When not to use ICT

- When developing skills with new instruments.
- To the exclusion of more traditional performance techniques.

Issues

- Balancing the development of ICT skills and musical learning.
- Opportunities for teachers to develop ICT skills.
- Having to 'build in' musicality to computer-created work.
- Integrating ICT with established class learning methods.

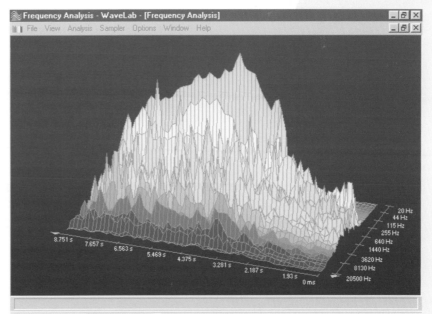

Further Information

The benefits of ICT in subject teaching
Objectives in the use of ICT
Assessing the use of ICT
Using the Internet
Using ICT to find things out
Automatic functions (1): control

Standards

2

Trainees must be taught how to use ICT most effectively in relation to subject-related objectives, including:

a. using ICT because it is the most effective way to achieve teaching and learning objectives, not simply to motivate pupils or as a reward or sanction for good or poor work or behaviour;

b. avoiding the use of ICT for simple or routine tasks which would be better accomplished by other means;

c. knowing that, where ICT is to be used, appropriate preparation of equipment, content and methodology is required;

d. avoiding giving the impression that the quality of presentation is of overriding importance and supersedes the importance of content;

e. structuring pupils' work to focus on relevant aspects and to maximise use of time and resource;

f. having high expectations of the outcomes of pupils' work with ICT, including:
   - expecting pupils to use ICT to answer valid questions appropriate to the subject matter being taught;
   - when appropriate, requiring pupils to save work, and evaluate and improve it;

g. making explicit the links between:
   i the ICT application and the subject matter it is being used to teach;
   ii ICT and its impact on everyday applications.

17

Trainees must demonstrate that they know how each of the following is relevant to the specialist subject and phase for which they are training:

a. **generic procedures and tools**, including
   i. understanding the key features and functions used within the subject;
   ii. using ICT to prepare material for pupil use.

b. **reference resources**, including;
   i. how to search reference resources;
   ii. how to incorporate the use of reference resources into teaching.

c. **the ICT specific to the subject;**

d. **the major teaching programs or "courseware" to ensure that material is matched to the pupils' competences;**

When the Statutory Order for IT in the National Curriculum was produced in 1995, Physical Education was the only subject which did not have an obligation to contribute to pupils' IT capability. The new standards for ICT in subject teaching recognise that Physical Education, alongside all other subjects, can benefit from the potential of the new technologies to enhance teaching and learning.

The use of ICT in Physical Education can be looked at under three headings: Planning, Performance and Evaluation.

Planning

Plans can be drawn up using a drawing or word processing program for the layout of activity areas or fitness routines designed by pupils. Once saved, amendments can be made when the routines have been tried and tested. Ideas might include circuit training activities, rules for small-sided team games and when older pupils are designing activities for younger ones, the layout of equipment. Attention will need to be paid to the presentation, use of language/pictures, and use of colour if the designs are to be used by other pupils.

The Internet can be used for research into sports organisations, skills and techniques. Links with national sports organisations, coaching facilities, rules, etc. can be obtained from link lists such as **www.schoolzone.co.uk**. (Physical Education and Sport).

E-mail can make it easy to arrange and confirm fixtures, contact outside organisations for information, or to link pupils in one school with those in another, to exchange ideas, views and information.

Performance

Traditionally stopwatches, timers and measuring tapes have been part of pupils' experience in Physical Education activities. Applications of ICT in Physical Education now incorporate the use of sensing equipment to measure pupil performance: heart rate monitors, blood pressure measurement, temperature sensors, work rate monitors and metabolic gas analysis. These are now within the reach of secondary schools.

CD-ROMs, databases and the Internet can provide resources for learning a new activity, techniques for improving performance or background information on events, past and present sports and sports people which can be useful for research and project work.

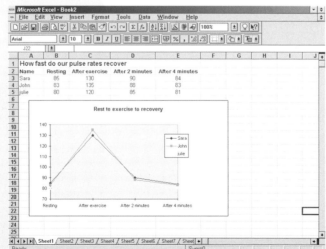

Video is particularly useful to develop observational and analysis skills. Slow motion and freeze frame functions can help improve kinesthetic awareness by allowing events to be watched repeatedly.

Spreadsheets and databases enable analytical work to be carried out on data collected during sports activities. This can encourage pupils to look for patterns and relationships using functions such as sort, mean, standard deviation and finally to display the results.

Evaluation

Pupils can use the graphs/data to monitor their own performance in particular areas and set themselves targets for the future. For example, progress in an area such as swimming can be recorded as badges for distance or skills are acquired. If each pupil has their user area on a network they can save a record of their development in the school – a Sports Skills Profile for their achievements.

Theory

For the theoretical aspects of the GCSE, A-level and GNVQ, the Internet has up-to-date resources on all aspects of the syllabus. CD-ROMs can provide detailed tutorials on the human body systems, dietary analysis programs and fitness tests allowing modelling of particular training regimes.

At a professional level

ICT can have an impact on day-to-day school administration and assessment systems, rotas and timetables for the use of equipment, hall space, playground, etc. These can be reproduced for all staff, including supply teachers. Sports days, galas and tournaments demand a high level of organisation and communication. ICT applications such as word processors and spreadsheets are particularly useful in minimising the administrative burden.

Fitness profile

Pupils in Year 7 prepared a personal fitness profile during a unit on the theme of fitness. As part of normal Physical Education lessons, pupils recorded their pulse rates at rest, after walking for three minutes (both with and without a heavy school bag), and after jogging for three minutes (if possible, carrying the school bag). The results were recorded on a teacher-prepared worksheet. Next lesson, the pupils entered their results into a database file, where they were stored for future retrieval. Later lessons in the sequence covered breathing, exercise targets and recovery rates – all entailing practical recording of results and subsequent adding of the data to the existing fitness profile database.

Fitness test sites on the Web were compared with techniques used in school.

The results were stored to support personal targets and for improvement purposes, since they would regularly be returning to aspects of personal fitness in their work in Physical Education.

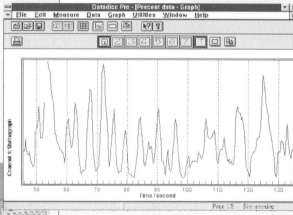

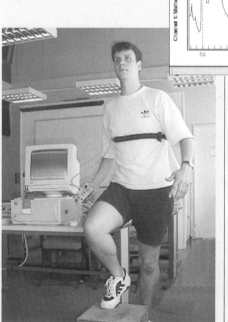

Further Information

The benefits of ICT in subject teaching
Objectives in the use of ICT
Assessing the use of ICT
Using spreadsheet software
Using database software
Automatic functions (2): sensing

Standards

2

Trainees must be taught how to use ICT most effectively in relation to subject-related objectives, including:

a. using ICT because it is the most effective way to achieve teaching and learning objectives, not simply to motivate pupils or as a reward or sanction for good or poor work or behaviour;

b. avoiding the use of ICT for simple or routine tasks which would be better accomplished by other means;

c. knowing that, where ICT is to be used, appropriate preparation of equipment, content and methodology is required;

d. avoiding giving the impression that the quality of presentation is of overriding importance and supersedes the importance of content;

e. structuring pupils' work to focus on relevant aspects and to maximise use of time and resource;

f. having high expectations of the outcomes of pupils' work with ICT, including:
   - expecting pupils to use ICT to answer valid questions appropriate to the subject matter being taught;
   - when appropriate, requiring pupils to save work, and evaluate and improve it;

g. making explicit the links between:
   i. the ICT application and the subject matter it is being used to teach;
   ii. ICT and its impact on everyday applications.

17

Trainees must demonstrate that they know how each of the following is relevant to the specialist subject and phase for which they are training:

a. **generic procedures and tools**, including
   i. understanding the key features and functions used within the subject;
   ii. using ICT to prepare material for pupil use.

b. **reference resources**, including;
   i. how to search reference resources;
   ii. how to incorporate the use of reference resources into teaching.

c. **the ICT specific to the subject;**

d. the major teaching programs or "courseware" to ensure that material is matched to the pupils' competences;

Using ICT in Religious Education provides one of the biggest challenges, but also the best opportunities to enhance pupil motivation, refresh resources and effect good learning. There is a mass of electronic information on, about and for religion. Some of it is very useful for teachers and their pupils.

Below are some of the ways in which RE teachers can use ICT resources:

- The use of word processing and DTP to enable the learner and practitioner to examine the response of individuals to religious experience through the drafting and writing of prayers, faith stories, retelling in a modern idiom of parables and the interpretation of religious writings.

- The use of multimedia and sound technology to promote the development of human relationships through the use of art, music, drama, story or word, focused on the praise and celebration of the life-giving force flowing from God/deity, e.g. the preparation of assemblies and collective worship.

- The use of encyclopedia and information-led packages to enable the learner and practitioner to benefit from past and present experiences and traditions of their faith, and the faith of others.

- The use of data-handling and spreadsheets to enable the learner and practitioner to celebrate the joys and challenges of their faith experiences.

- The use of the Internet and E-mail to communicate with other faith traditions and in doing so explore common values, attitudes and beliefs.

ICT in RE is, therefore, an essential tool and one in which teacher and pupil will collaborate in exploring its creative, bonding and empathic effects. It is not, however, an end in itself, and will not replace contemporary and practised methodologies. Rather it should be used to enrich and enhance best practice. If the teacher acknowledges these qualities of the partnership between RE and ICT in their lesson planning, the avenues for exploration are limitless and move beyond the word processing/desk-top publishing practice of producing and presenting work of a religious nature.

Resources

Learning is increasingly supported by resources from a multiplicity of media: text, videotext, audiotext, images, graphics, music, etc. Bringing such material to the classroom is facilitated by multimedia machines and connection to the Internet.

Searching for information on the Internet

Writing about RE often lags behind current practice and yet every religious organisation publishes itself on the World Wide Web. RE teachers need to have the skills to search the 'Net', for materials that can best enhance the quality of their teaching.

There are those who wish to fill the Internet with their particular form of religious mania. Quality control is therefore perhaps more critical in this subject than any other. A careless search can hit on some rather unsavoury material under the guise of religion. Always produce closed tasks which you know will get your pupils to places only you want them to go.

Searching is an essential skill for Bible study both on the Internet and using the variety of digital versions of the Bible.

Multimedia packages like *Encarta* or *Compton's Interactive Encyclopedia*, which many pupils have at home bundled together by the company that supplied their home PC, can be used to supplement resources on many of the world's religions.

RE-NET

In partnership with Canterbury Christ Church University College, St. Simon Stock School in Maidstone have created a Web site for RE teachers. The site consists of classroom resources, reference material and links to other Web sites of interest to R.E. teachers.
www.cant.ac.uk/renet

Teaching with ICT

Art, graphics and presentation packages such as *Microsoft Powerpoint* can be used to allow pupils to make personal responses to the stimulus material that is so abundant in Religious Education. Art and graphics packages can become the tools for exploring symbolic representation. DTP can assist in the production of banners, invitations, posters, flash cards and notices which can all stimulate learning and personal response. Pupils of all abilities can be given the responsibility to create one part of a whole class presentation or wall display.

Data-handling

Data-handling packages have become essential tools for collaborative group work. Investigations undertaken during the 'recognise and reflect' stage of a programme of study can be facilitated by the use of computers. This provides a marvellous way to engage and encourage the learner to share their own personal experiences, to discover, to make comparisons with, to acknowledge, and to respect their neighbours' different faith traditions. Data can be collected using older technologies like tape recorders but the material gathered can be processed using spreadsheets or databases.

Further Information

The benefits of ICT in subject teaching
Objectives in the use of ICT
Assessing the use of ICT
Using word processing software
Communicating information
Using ICT to find things out

Modelling

Modelling packages and some computer games can help pupils experience the wider world issues of poverty, consequences of war, and political decisions on justice and peace. In role, and spurred on by the need to win, they will engage in decision making and considering the consequences of those decisions. Careful

selection of the game, time management and reporting back will provide interesting discussion points where value systems can be challenged and articulated. This can provide a particularly stimulating activity for reluctant learners.

Image captured with digital camera

Gawdawpalin temple, near Pagan, Burma. Built in the reign of Narapatisithu (1174-1211) The top of the stupa was 55 metres high when built.

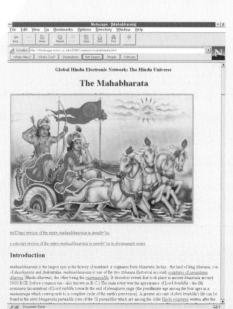

Standards

8

In order to understand how to monitor, evaluate and assess their teaching and pupils' learning in the subject when using ICT, and to evaluate the contribution that ICT has made to the teaching of their subject, trainees must be taught:

a. how to **monitor pupils' progress** by:
   i. being clear about teaching objectives and the use of ICT in achieving them;
   ii. observing and intervening in pupils' ICT-based activities to monitor and support their progression towards the identified objectives;
   iii. asking key questions which require pupils to reflect on the appropriateness of their use of ICT;

b. **how to recognise standards of attainment in the subject** when ICT resources are used, including:
   i. recognising how access to computer functions might change teacher expectation of pupil achievements;
   ii. identifying criteria by which pupils can show what they have learnt as a result of using ICT-based resources from the Internet or CD-ROM, and insisting that pupils acknowledge the reference sources used in their work;
   iii. how to determine the achievement of individuals when the "product" is the result of a collaborative effort, through observation, record keeping, teacher intervention and pupil-teacher dialogue;
   iv. how to ensure that assessment of ICT-based work reflects pupils' learning and the quality of their work within the subject(s) rather than just the quality of presentation or the complexity of the technology used;

c. how to use **formative, diagnostic and summative methods of assessing pupils' progress in the subject where ICT has been used**, including how to set up ICT activities with targeted objectives for assessment and make provision in those activities for all pupils to demonstrate achievement, conceptual understanding and learning through the use of ICT.

Teachers use assessment as part of teaching and learning. Intuitively they assess pupils' progress and adjust strategies accordingly. Using new technology can make teachers anxious and this can make assessment seem more onerous than it is in their specialist areas of the curriculum.

ICT raises a variety of issues when assessing pupils' attainment and progress in the subject.

The value of presentation

Teachers' unfamiliarity with ICT can create problems when assessing pupils' level of attainment. The use of ICT can easily mask pupil performance. In many subjects ICT is used as a tool for improving the quality of presentation. It is easy to think that a word processed document, lavishly illustrated with colourful clipart is superior to a hand-written one! Beyond the fact that it might be easier to read, it might not only b᠎ activity set, but also an inappropri᠎

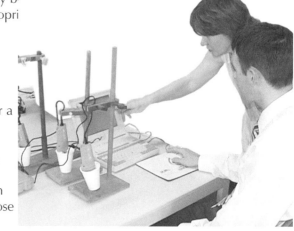

In other activities a more professional mode of presentation might be, for example, producing an advertising leaflet in English, or a formal report of a field-trip in Geography. Teachers need to consider if pupils demonstrate that they had design criteria which they worked towards, in terms of a clear sense of purpose and the target audience.

Using electronic sources

Printing out a page from *Microsoft Encarta* with its illustrations is no more valuable than a page copied by hand from a paper-based encyclopedia. Both products fail to show that the learner has done more than accessed the source and raises concerns about the learning that has taken place. Here the teacher also needs to be aware of issues of authorship, i.e. the extent to which the writer has made the material their own, and that sources have been properly acknowledged.

Assessment procedures

Schools need to have effective assessment procedures in place which account for a pupil's developing skills in using ICT appropriately and for the way in which ICT improves the quality of outcome in terms of each subject. In particular, teachers need to develop the skills and confidence to be able to distinguish between assessing a pupil's progress in the subject area, and in the development of their IT capability. Diagnostic and formative assessment can be on the basis of observation and discussion as the teacher circulates. Written feedback can also be retrospectively based on printed material or saved files. It is necessary to ensure that pupils are able to print out their work on a regular basis or alternatively to submit files for the teacher to review and comment on.

Assessing group work

Group projects are a popular way of using ICT resources: the best computer-based tasks promote debate and collaboration. For example, pupils acting as journalists research information at an individual level and then submit their articles for inclusion. However, here there is some difficulty with assessing individuals' contributions. Careful observation and periodic reviews can help identify individual progress, and requiring pupils to keep a log of their developments can help the teacher make a sound summative judgement.

Recording progress

Pupils could be encouraged to add their own evaluative comments when submitting group work produced with ICT.

- What were the advantages in using ICT for this task?
- What IT skills did you use to achieve this result?
- What new IT skills did you have to acquire?
- What other ways could you have achieved a similar outcome without the use of ICT?

In planning a unit of work the subject teacher will need to consider the ICT dimension of the work when giving thought to summative assessment exercises.

Setting targets

Pupils need to be informed about their particular strengths and weaknesses in relation to ICT. The more they become aware of the specific things they need to achieve in order to make progress, the more likely they are to achieve them. As in other subjects, pupils need to have clear targets for improvement in their IT capability.

In setting up ICT activities a teacher might clarify the specific opportunities to perform in various aspects of IT at different levels. In speaking to an individual pupil a teacher might reinforce the fact that simply going to an electronic source and printing off the material may be progress, whereas with another pupil the teacher might prompt a critical evaluation of the content.

Monitoring assessment practice

Analysis of data derived from assessment will reveal how different groups of pupils are making progress, and give rise to a series of questions. Do girls (in a mixed school) compete for the resources equally with the boys during lessons? Are the attitudes of boys and girls different to using the technology outside directed lessons? Stereotypically, boys are often initially motivated by the use of computers, which are viewed as a suitably masculine pursuit. Girls are often more pragmatic and will evaluate the use of ICT against a set of objectives which may include criteria that appear to have little relevance to the technology. Indeed, do all pupils have equal access to ICT resources? Access at home is increasing (though often used predominantly for games!): how can the teacher make allowance for this? Is positive discrimination sometimes desirable?

Key questions

- What do I expect from the inclusion of ICT in my lesson/scheme of work?
- What subject objectives have I identified in my planning?
- How are the pupils likely to interpret my instructions?
- What outcomes could pupils produce?
- How will different pupils' ability influence the outcomes?
- How can I differentiate the support I give?
- What criteria will I use to mark/evaluate the outcomes?
- What feedback will I give to the pupils?
- How will I communicate the feedback?

Things to do

Look around the school ICT resources at lunchtime. In a co-educational environment what is the balance of boys and girls using the computers?

What are the pupils doing? Is there a difference between the two sexes' use of ICT applications?

Further information

Lesson planning
The benefits of ICT in subject teaching
Objectives in the use of IT

Standards

12

Trainees must demonstrate that they are competent in those areas of ICT which support pedagogy in every subject, including that they:

a. can employ common ICT tools for their own and pupils' benefit, and can use a range of ICT resources, at the level of general users (rather than as network or system managers), including:

   i. the common user interfaces, using menus, selecting and swapping between applications, cutting, pasting and copying files, and cutting copying and pasting data within and between applications;

   ii. successfully connecting and setting up ICT equipment, including input devices;

   iii. loading and running software;

   iv. file management;

   v. seeking and using operating information, including from on-line help facilities and user guides;

   vi. coping with everyday problems and undertaking simple, routine maintenance, with due consideration to health and safety;

   vii. understanding the importance of passwords and the general security of equipment and access to it and ensuring that it works;

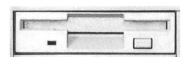

CD-ROM drive
Used for reading or loading information by the CPU. Unlike the floppy disk information cannot be written onto the CD, however it can contain over 650 MB of information as opposed to the 1.4 MB of the diskette.

Floppy disk drive
Used for loading or storing information on a 3.5 inch diskette.

VDU (visual display unit) or Monitor
The screen which displays the information from the computer. Most are colour and fully adjustable.

CPU (central processing-unit) or Processor
Controls all the information and executes all the commands.

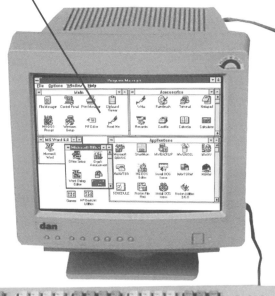

Keyboard
Set out as a conventional typewriter with some extra keys, this is used to give commands to the computer by typing or pressing combinations of keys.

Mouse
This is used to move an arrow or pointer around the screen in order to select various command options or activate options from the menu bar.

Digital camera
Similar to a conventional camera this captures images in a digital format instead of on film, ready for use with the computer.

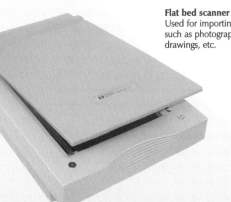

Flat bed scanner
Used for importing images such as photographs, drawings, etc.

Ink jet printer
Used for printing out information from the computer in text or graphic format.

Three-pin plugs and sockets
Used to supply power to the computer and VDU.

Five-pin DIN plug
Connects the keyboard to the CPU.

Fifteen-pin D-type plug
Connects the VDU to the CPU.

Parallel cable
The two ends are different. One is a 25 Pin D-type male, for use in the parallel port (RS232) The other is a parallel D-type which plugs into the back of the printer.

Nine-pin D-type socket
Connects the mouse to the CPU.

Standards

12

Trainees must demonstrate that they are competent in those areas of ICT which support pedagogy in every subject, including that they:

a. can employ common ICT tools for their own and pupils' benefit, and can use a range of ICT resources, at the level of general users (rather than as network or system managers), including:

   i. the common user interfaces, using menus, selecting and swapping between applications, cutting, pasting and copying files, and cutting copying and pasting data within and between applications;

   ii. successfully connecting and setting up ICT equipment, including input devices;

   iii. loading and running software;

   iv. file management;

   v. seeking and using operating information, including from on-line help facilities and user guides;

   vi. coping with everyday problems and undertaking simple, routine maintenance, with due consideration to health and safety;

   vii. understanding the importance of passwords and the general security of equipment and access to it, and ensuring that it works.

The computer or network's operating system enables files to be effectively organised for maximum efficiency and ease of use.

Running installed programs

Teachers and pupils in the classroom generally run programs that are already installed and ready to use. Double-clicking with the mouse on the program icon opens it.

Using new software

A new program will be supplied on one or more floppy disks, or more commonly on a CD-ROM. It is sometimes possible to run a program directly from the floppy disk or CD-ROM, but usually the software is copied and installed to the hard drive of the computer or network server. To aid the user in installing a new program the software provides an executable file (e.g. *Winword.exe*). This has the instructions for the installation, and can be activated using the **Run** option from the **File Menu** in the **Program Manager** menu in *Windows 3.1,* or the **Start** menu of *Windows '95.*

The installation program will usually provide straightforward instructions so the software can be installed in a few simple steps. Some of these steps will require information to be provided about the system that the program is being installed on.

CD-ROMs are straightforward to install. The operation is often done automatically when the disk is inserted. If not, the instructions provided with the CD-ROM box should be followed.

Handling Files

The principles of handling files in *Windows 3.1* are essentially the same as in *Windows '95.* The illustrations below refer specifically to *Windows 3.1.*

Amongst other things, using **File Manager** in *Windows 3.1* will:

- Install new software
- Create new directories
- Move and Copy files
- Format floppy disks ready for use
- Provide information about files, e.g. their size and date created

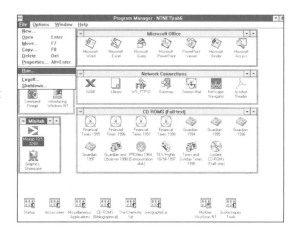

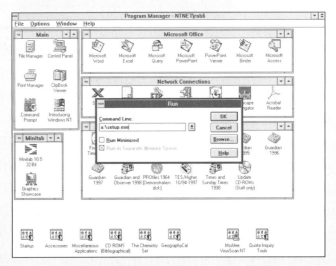

Across the top of the screen is a set of icons that represent the different 'drives' that are accessible. These drives provide access to memory that may be on a floppy disk, on a hard drive inside the computer itself, or on a network 'server'. Selecting a drive will show all the directories and their contents.

Directories

Good housekeeping of files can save time and ensure work is not lost. Directories are labelled areas where files can be stored together, similar to the way that papers are organised in files in a filing cabinet. New directories can be created in **File Manager**

Moving Files

Files can be moved or copied within all the directories, and to or from the different drives. This can be achieved through the **File** menu or using a 'drag and drop' method.

Some other useful functions in **File Manager** are backing up files, renaming files and deleting files.

Help

Extensive on-line help is available in *Windows* and within other *Windows* applications. There are a number of search strategies to help the user find information on most topics.

Drives
Usually:
Drive A:\ is for accessing memory on a floppy disk.
Drive C:\ is for accessing memory on the hard disk in the computer.
Drive N:\ is the network drive, within which are specific directories used to store users' files.
Drive P:\ is the public drive on a network where users can access files but cannot alter or save to the area.

There will be other drives with letters which are unique to the set up of the machine or network.

In the classroom

- Direct the pupils to an area where they are able to access files, e.g. the P:\ drive. When pupils save their work it will usually be to the C:\ or N:\ drive or the A:\ floppy disk drive. Confidently accessing drives is a skill all teachers need!

- Be able to sort out problems with directories and subdirectories for pupils.

- Load programs from a floppy disk or CD-ROM and run them (with appropriate approval from IT co-ordinators, etc.)

- Know how to set up a printer on a stand-alone or laptop computer.

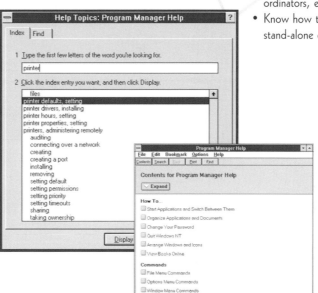

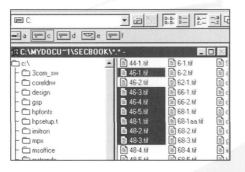

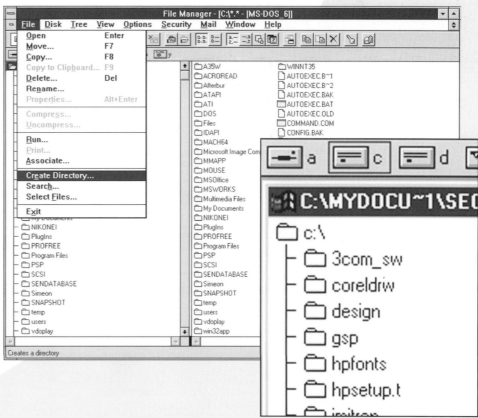

Standards

12

Trainees must demonstrate that they are competent in those areas of ICT which support pedagogy in every subject, including that they:

a. can employ common ICT tools for their own and pupils' benefit, and can use a range of ICT resources, at the level of general users (rather than as network or system managers), including:

   i. the common user interfaces, using menus, selecting and swapping between applications, cutting, pasting and copying files, and cutting copying and pasting data within and between applications;

   ii. successfully connecting and setting up ICT equipment, including input devices;

   iii. loading and running software;

   iv. file management;

   v. seeking and using operating information, including from on-line help facilities and user guides;

   vi. coping with everyday problems and undertaking simple, routine maintenance, with due consideration to health and safety;

   vii. understanding the importance of passwords and the general security of equipment and access to it, and ensuring that it works.

> *'It's important that you spend some time getting to know how to use the interface. Be warned that some pupils will be experts and will know how to change the way the interface looks and works. Ask the IT co-ordinator or technician what has been done to prevent this happening.'*

The user interface is what makes it possible for someone to interact with the computer. This is the screen that the user sees when the operating system has loaded after starting the computer.

Modern computers have a 'graphical user interface' (GUI) which presents the user with different icons, buttons, menus, dialogue boxes that make it easier to operate the computer.

The most common GUI is the *Windows* system, produced by the Microsoft Corporation. There is more than one version of Windows. Each version of *Windows* looks slightly different from the other, and is used in different ways. There are significant differences between a *Windows '95* user interface and earlier versions such as *Windows 3.1*. The GUI of operating systems of an Apple Macintosh or an Acorn Archimedes also look different, but many of the principles are similar. It is essential to know which GUI is being used and to be familiar with its main features.

Once the basic features of the GUI are mastered, similarities will be found in other applications running within that interface. This helps provide a familiar environment in which to learn how to use new applications.

Using the interface

The prime function within the **Program Manager** of *Windows 3.1* is to allow the user to quickly and easily start up, and close, programs such as a word processor or spreadsheet. The small pictures on the Program Manager screen are called 'icons'. Each represents a computer program. The icons are usually placed together in different **Program Groups**. In *Windows '95* the **Program Manager** is replaced by a **My Compute**r function which also has icon groups.

Generally the programs in the GUI are accessed using the mouse to move a cursor about on the screen. Selecting an item within the GUI is achieved with a 'click' of the left hand mouse button. To start a program requires a 'double click'. Drop-down menus require a single click to open them and another to select an option. **Dialogue boxes** provide information about what actions the computer is taking, and may require a response from the user via the keyboard.

Windows can be resized by clicking on and dragging the sides of the boxes to a new size. Alternatively any **Program Group** can be maximised and minimised.

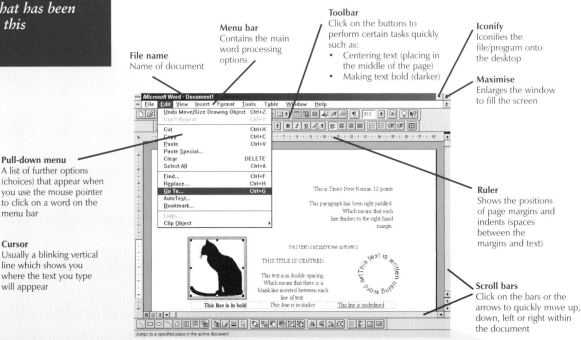

Menu bar
Contains the main word processing options

Toolbar
Click on the buttons to perform certain tasks quickly such as:
- Centering text (placing in the middle of the page)
- Making text bold (darker)

Iconify
Iconifies the file/program onto the desktop

Maximise
Enlarges the window to fill the screen

File name
Name of document

Pull-down menu
A list of further options (choices) that appear when you use the mouse pointer to click on a word on the menu bar

Cursor
Usually a blinking vertical line which shows you where the text you type will apppear

Ruler
Shows the positions of page margins and indents (spaces between the margins and text)

Scroll bars
Click on the bars or the arrows to quickly move up, down, left or right within the document

Switching between programs

Computers can run more than one program at a time. This is known as multi-tasking. Selecting any part of an open program's window using the mouse will make it active. This allows the user to move quickly between different applications. Another method, using the keyboard, is to hold down the **Alt** key, and then press and release the **Tab** key. This brings up a window which enables the user to move through a list of open program items. Releasing the **Alt** key selects the highlighted program.

Material from one open file can be **copied** to an area known as the **clipboard** and then **pasted** into another open file from a different program. Files and data from two different programs can also be linked together so that automatic updating of either document can be made.

In practice

Being familiar with the GUI is vital for teachers.

'Sir, I've lost the scroll bar at the bottom!'

If pupils can change the style and layout of the GUI they will! The results of 'customising' can be disconcerting for an unsuspecting teacher. Usually pupils either cannot make changes or save changes when the computer is closed down. Check out the system access arrangements and keep backup copies of vital system files.

'Miss, I've lost my work!'

Maximising and minimising program windows can be very confusing and pupils sometimes think their work is lost. The computer will complain about lack of memory if too many programs are open and crashes will be generally avoided automatically.

In the classroom

- Use the interface confidently.
- Load and use any software package showing expertise in the use of the interface.
- Make changes to the files used to store work demonstrating advanced interface skills, such as deleting or renaming files, or copying them to new storage locations.
- Customise the computer display, retrieve accidentally deleted files, or protect work from being altered by pupils.

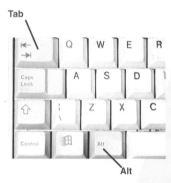

*Use the **Alt** and **Tab** keys to quickly switch betwen programs or files*

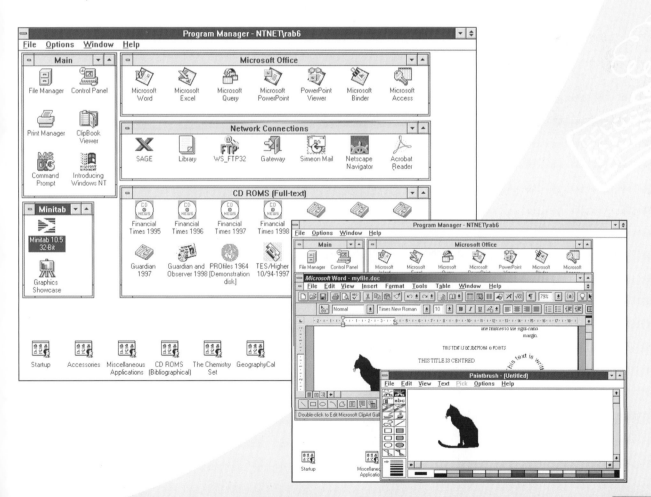

Using ICT

Standards

5

Trainees must be taught to recognise the specific contribution that ICT can make to teaching pupils with special educational needs in mainstream classrooms based upon the need to:

a. provide access to the curriculum in a manner appropriate to pupils' needs;

b. provide subject-specific support.

15

Trainees must demonstrate that they are aware of the potential of ICT to enable them to prepare and present their teaching more effectively, taking account of:

a. the intended audience, including matching and adapting work to subject matter and objectives, pupils' prior attainment, reading ability or special educational needs; recognising the efficiency with which such adaptations can be made using ICT;

b. the most appropriate forms of presentation to meet teaching objectives,

The keyboard and the mouse are the main ways in which computers can be controlled. A range of alternative input devices are available to meet users different needs and preferences.

Mice are available in many different shapes and sizes. On laptops the mouse has been replaced by touch pads. Mainstream manufacturers have complemented the work of specialist companies working to ensure the inclusion of people with more specialised needs.

Touch screens

Touch screens are devices which enable a user to control a computer by pointing to or touching an area of the screen. Most touch screens use a clear plastic window placed in front of a standard monitor. However, touch screens built into monitors are now becoming very reliable. They should work with any mouse-driven software, but it must be 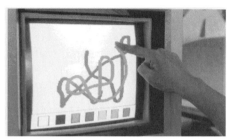 remembered that mouse-driven programs are designed for small cursors rather than large fingers so, although it is a very direct method of access, some pupils may not be able to locate the precise, often small, areas required. The touch screen has advantages especially when used with multimedia. With some interactive talking books, learners can point at a word and then hear it spoken.

Overlay keyboards

Another means of accessing the computer is by using an overlay keyboard, also known as a membrane or 'Concept Keyboard'. This is a flat board with a matrix of touch sensitive keys. This matrix may consist of over a hundred keys, up to more than 4000, depending upon the type of overlay keyboard. A paper overlay is placed on top of this keyboard so that when the pupil presses an area, the computer responds to the message assigned to the area.

Overlay keyboards can often be used alongside standard QWERTY keyboards. This is particularly useful for students who cannot use a standard keyboard or find it laborious. Overlays can be prepared with whole words and phrases assigned to areas so that pupils can write text in the normal way. Whole words or chunks of pre-prepared text can be inserted by pressing a sector of the pad, saving the physical or intellectual effort of typing every word letter by letter.

Keyguards

Keyguards are available for most keyboards. They are inexpensive and guide a keyboard user who may have poor hand co-ordination. This can be used alongside predicting software and 'sticky key' software.

Mini Keyboards

This is a very small keyboard which may be of use to someone with very limited range of hand/finger movement and possibly little strength to press keys. The keys are arranged around a central space key according to frequency rather than the more usual 'QWERTY' format. Alternatively, an 'organiser' or palm top computer may be of use.

Alternative Mice

All mice work on the same principle - a rolling ball makes a cursor move around the screen and selections are made by pressing the buttons on the mouse. The ball is usually underneath the mouse and is controlled by moving it across the surface. If a pupil finds using a mouse difficult, some programs and operating systems allow keyboard alternatives to be used. There are also mouse key access utilities available that transfer the vertical, horizontal and diagonal movements of the mouse to other keys, such as the numeric keypad, e.g., *Easy Access* on the Macintosh, *Special Access* on the Acorn and the PC.

A number of variants to the mouse are available with different shapes and sizes of body and buttons, including a mouse that looks a bit like the real animal! These fit the conventional port and software programs.

Trackerballs are basically upside-down mice where a mounted ball is moved by the hand. It means that less gross hand and arm movement is required. A large trackerball with a billiard-sized ball, plus an extra middle button, is available. Some trackerballs have control over x and y movement, plus extra toggle switches for holding the left and right buttons down. They are also available as joysticks or as a foot operated trackerball.

The 'trackerball' is designed to facilitate access, by allowing switches to replace the actions of the mouse buttons, and can temporarily 'lock' into vertical or horizontal movement.

The Ball Point Mouse is a portable mouse which can be mounted on the edge of a notebook keyboard and controlled by the thumb and first finger or held in the palm of a hand. The Microsoft *Easy Ball* is a very large trackerball intended for younger learners who may have difficulties in co-ordinating the movement of a mouse.

Other alternatives include a stylus used with a graphics tablet, and a mouse pen. These will be of limited use for people with gross and fine motor movement in the arm or hand.

Mouse keys enable the keyboard arrows to pretend to be a mouse. This is standard on Macintosh computers but is readily available on other computers. It can be very useful for someone who uses a head pointer or key-guard who might find it difficult or impossible to use a mouse.

Improving access on the PC

The way the mouse moves is affected by the surface it rests on. Mouse mats can be made with a resistance that suits the user. The relationship between the distance that the cursor moves in the screen and the distance that the mouse moves across the work surface is called the 'mouse speed', and can be altered in most computers through their configuration or control panels, or by additional access utilities. As well as moving the cursor around the screen, the pupil needs to make selections by clicking the mouse switch button. This causes a problem for pupils who cannot reach the switch buttons, or who cannot press them without moving the mouse.

One way of overcoming this problem is to connect the buttons to a separate switch through a mouse/switch box.

Some programs require the pupil to press the switch twice in a given space of time in order to make a selection. This 'double-clicking' may cause difficulties if the student cannot make the second press in the time allowed.

The maximum time allowed between clicks is called the 'double-click speed' and most computers provide a way of adjusting this through their configuration or control panels, but if this is still not long enough manufacturers should be able to give information on extending it even further.

Some mice have extra buttons which can have functions such as 'double-click' allocated to them.

Another mouse action that pupils may often need is 'click and drag' - holding the button down at the same time as moving the mouse. It is used to draw lines in painting programs or to move items from one place to another. If the 'click and drag' action presents problems, a 'latching' mouse or trackerball can be used, which enables the pupil to lock the switch button on while moving the mouse, then release it again when the cursor has reached its destination.

Standards

15

Trainees must demonstrate that they are aware of the potential of ICT to enable them to prepare and present their teaching more effectively, taking account of:

a. the intended audience, including matching and adapting work to subject matter and objectives, pupils' prior attainment, reading ability or special educational needs; recognising the efficiency with which such adaptations can be made using ICT;

b. the most appropriate forms of presentation to meet teaching objectives.

17

Trainees must demonstrate that they know how each of the following is relevant to the specialist subject and phase for which they are training:

d. the major teaching programs or "courseware" to ensure that material is matched to the pupils' competences;

   i. where content and activities are presented in sequence to teach specific topics;

   ii. where teaching activities are combined with assessment tasks and tests.

CD-ROM, the Internet and powerful computers running on fast networks have made possible the development of computer-based courseware which facilitates pupils working independently.

Developments in flexible learning

Flexible learning resources do not of necessity require a computer. The Open University has been very influential in developing the use of a range of media to support independent learning at Higher Education level. Paper-based materials are combined with audio-tapes, video and television programmes, computer-based tasks and, more recently, video-conferencing. The development of flexible learning resources in schools has predominantly been at A-level and more recently to support GNVQ studies. A good deal of the initiative for flexible learning in the UK has come from the development of distance learning in areas such as Wales and Scotland and the South West, where distance and demography make it difficult to meet the needs of the population locally. However, nationally schools have become interested in the potential of Intranet and Internet resources to provide for the needs of particular groups or courses within the institution.

ICT-based flexible learning in schools

ICT flexible learning resources in schools may include:

- CD-ROM based systems, e.g. to support Modern Language teaching.

- Internet based systems, e.g. revision resources for Mathematics and English.

- Paper and other media resources, e.g. for basic skills in Mathematics.

- Intranet resources materials created by the school for use internally but delivered via a Web browser such as *Netscape*. Alternatively these materials can be purchased commercially.

- Integrated learning systems (ILS), generally used to teach skills in the core subjects.

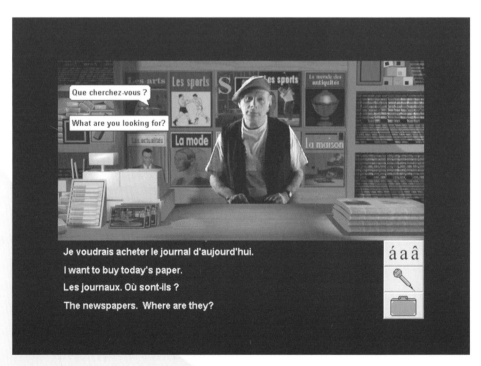

Integrated learning systems (ILS)

An ILS is a computer-based learning system which manages the delivery of curriculum materials to produce individual learning programmes. Learning within the ILS is supported by video and sound. They are generally used by schools to raise achievement in literacy and numeracy. Substantial improvements have been reported in individual pupils' progress in aspects of literacy and numeracy, but without a significant degree of reproducibility. ILS do, however, manage to diagnose difficulties, analyse progress and produce reports for pupils, parents and teachers. An increase in pupil motivation also appears to be inherent in the use of the system. Individual pupil progress is monitored through a reporting system and the programme of study adjusted accordingly.

Not all products have the same features of scope, cost or pattern of implementation in the classroom. There is some confusion over the use of the term ILS, which makes comparisons between systems difficult.

Evaluating the use of ILS

Benefits:

- Immediate feedback – no waiting for the teacher or work to be marked.

- Failing in private – no one else will know that the answer was wrong.

- The option exists to get the answer right the second time around.

- Differentiation – pupils can work at their own level.

- Pupils with disabilities can access higher levels without the need to read lengthy texts or having to worry about writing with poor motor skills. Text can be read to pupils with poor reading skills.

- Quality time with the teacher – using the ILS could free time for the teacher to work with smaller groups of pupils.

- Detailed reports on progress – individual pupils can be targeted and programmes adjusted to gain maximum achievement.

- Attendance can increase as pupils begin to feel successful and gain in confidence.

Disadvantages:

- The cost!

- Investment in time for training, the timetable and support staff is necessary to enable the system to be successful.

- There may be errors and 'bugs' in the system.

- Lack of adaptability – the system may provide too rigid a structure. Pupils may not understand the instructions. The pace can't be varied.

- Voices may be American and difficult to understand. American spellings are used in some systems.

- Concerns over a lack of development of higher order skills.

Evidence is emerging from evaluation of the use of ILS that the context in which the system is used is a determining factor in its effectiveness. The material and approach in the subject area it supports needs to reinforce concepts and skills in mainstream classwork.

Things to do

- Find out what flexible learning resources are in use.
- Find out if the school uses ILS and how pupils are given access. The SENCO or the literacy and numeracy co-ordinators will be useful people to talk to. Which pupils have access?
- Investigate whether the claims for achievement are valid. Do reading ages improve dramatically? Ask to see some evidence and look at the printouts of the reports. Try to observe pupils at work. Do pupils find the 'success' motivating?
- Find out what support staff are required to enable flexible learning systems to be effective i.e. IT technician, classroom assistant, etc. What role do teachers play in a flexible learning environment?

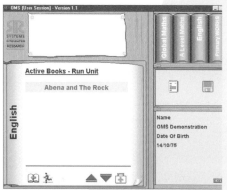

Further Information

Literacy and ICT
Numeracy and ICT
SEN and ICT
ICT in English
ICT in Mathematics

Standards

6

Trainees must be taught how to choose and use the most suitable ICT to meet teaching objectives, by reviewing a range of generic and subject-specific software critically, including how to:

a. assess its potential for helping to meet teaching objectives;

b. judge its suitability for the age of pupils, their stage of development, and their prior experiences, taking account of language, social and cultural background;

c. evaluate the success of its use in relation to teaching objectives.

> - **Is the software to be used on a network or stand-alone computer?**
> - **How much time is available for pupils to use it?**
> - **What support will have to be available (on-line help, classroom assistants, worksheets)?**
> - **What is the previous experience/skills of the pupils?**
> - **What is the curriculum context in which the software is to be used?**

There are very few places where teachers can go to find an independent and critical evaluation of software. For teachers to exploit the potential of software in the curriculum they need to be aware of the software's features and/or content 'intentions' and match these to the learning activity.

It is useful to remember that, with a few exceptions, software is designed for the user rather than for purposes of teaching and learning. The human-computer interface within the software is designed to engage with the needs of the user at a number of levels of capability.

Generic software and specific software

It is important to be clear whether the software is a data handling tool (e.g. *Microsoft Access*), or a content rich source (e.g. a CD-ROM on musical instruments).

Generic applications, such as word processing, spreadsheet or database packages, are essentially supplied as content-free creative tools. However the teacher can use them to deliver content created by themselves or a provider. Data files turn generic applications into content resources. For example, *Pinpoint* is a survey tool used to support questionnaire production which builds a database as survey results are added. This software can also be used as a database to explore data files already assembled, e.g. on 'The Victorians'.

The interface of many generic applications can also be customised by the teacher or a supplier. For example, *Microsoft Word* can be simplified for younger pupils, or pupils with special educational needs, by enlarging and simplifying the icons and menus.

Templates can be used to structure work for pupils. *Microsoft Publisher* is a desk top publishing package which comes with a stimulating set of template designs for producing newspapers, leaflets, posters, etc.

Specific software is far more likely to be written for a learning context, such as a CD-ROM containing information on the Second World War.

Evaluation criteria

Ease of use/the interface

- How quickly can pupils work out how to use the main features?
- Are the icons and options self-explanatory? Will the interface be familiar to the pupils?
- Does the navigation system support independent use?
- Are the functions clear?
- How precise does the mouse control need to be?

Interactivity

- How easy is it to enter data or instructions?
- What sort of feedback does the user receive?
- Is customisation possible? (e.g. off-the-peg templates or data files, icons which can be enlarged or simplified)

Guidance

- How much specific support will pupils need to use the package?
- Does it come with any useful help files, manuals or supported self-study material?

Teaching and learning

- Are language and information appropriate to the pupils' developmental level?
- How long will it retain pupils' attention, interest and motivation?
- Does it have enough variety and possibilities to be used in a number of different ways?
- Is it relevant to the demands of the curriculum?
- Does the quality of the software encourage and facilitate higher quality teaching?
- Does it assist in teaching at the extremes of the ability range?

Technical robustness

- How quickly does it 'crash' if pupils try out different operations?
- Is it easy for pupils to find their way out of difficulties?

Things to do

- Review a piece of software or a CD-ROM using some of the evaluation criteria shown here.
- Share your reviews with other colleagues.
- Access the BECTa site shown here and find the CD-ROM evaluation materials.
- Locate the software reviews for your specialist subject.

Don Passey from Lancaster University suggests four key questions to assist in the process of evaluating the suitability and potential value of a piece of software:

- What type of learning activity does the software allow?
- What learning process does the software support?
- What management issues does the software present?
- Can the software be supported by the school's resources?

Netscape - [CD-ROM Evaluations]
File Edit View Go Bookmarks Options Directory Window
Netsite: http://www.becta.org.uk/projects/mmportables2/eval/evals/9100/9166.html
What's New? What's Cool? Destinations Net Search People Software

D/EE Department for Education and Employment

Multimedia Portable for Teachers

CD ROM Evaluation

Art Gallery

Hardware Platform(s):	Apple, PC
Publisher (where known):	
Average Unit Price:	£ 39.99
Curriculum Area(s):	Art

Date of Publication: 1994

Phase(s): KS2, KS3, KS4, Adult

Screen shots (click to enlarge)

Title screen

Example screens

Evaluators' comments

This disc contains 2,000 paintings from the National Gallery in London. It is extensive, well presented and informative. As well as looking at works of art, artists and historical settings, it also has information on which media have been used and how, and explanations of specialist terminology. It gets over the classroom management problem of having to store a lot of illustrations. It offers support to art teachers across all key stages as part of their continuing professional development; and provides a model of ways of looking at a gallery's collection, which could be transferred to a local collection.

It meets National Curriculum AT2 requirement as it allows pupils to identify different kinds of art and their purposes, within the restrictions of the National Gallery's collection. It would support art teachers across all key stages as part of their continuing professional development.

The script is aimed at adults, and the text contains the specialist vocabulary and sentence structure to match this audience. It could be useful to inform the non-specialist teacher, and the good upper KS2 reader and KS3 and KS4 students will be able to use it.

This is a user-friendly program that could be used by teachers and children with limited instruction and/or experience. The program is divided into five areas which are cross-referenced. The 'Guided Tours' section has a soundtrack which runs alongside the text and images, giving time to assimilate the information presented. The visual images are generally clear, and a number of them can be enlarged to illustrate pointers from the text.

Instructions for use are clear and easily understood, but the program itself is so easy that these are almost unnecessary.

This is a high-quality program that would be of value in both the primary and secondary sectors, being erudite and thorough.

Evaluation Date: March 1996

Supplier(s): Microsoft Ltd

Last update: 30 Oct 1997
New Search

Netscape

Further Information

Objectives in the use of ICT
SEN and ICT
Assessing the use of ICT

Becta home page

Standards

14

Trainees must demonstrate that they know those features of ICT which can be used, separately or together, to support teaching and learning in subjects, including:

c. **provisionality** - the function of ICT which allows changes to be made easily and enables alternatives to be explored readily, and as appropriate to the subject(s) and age of pupils to be taught:

 i. how to make best use of the ability to make rapid changes, including how to create text, designs and models which may be explored and improved in the light of evaluation;

 ii. how to judge when and when not to encourage exploration and change using ICT;

 iii. how saving work at different stages enables a record to be kept of the development of ideas;

 iv. how work can be improved through drafting and redrafting.

'Word processing at its best can improve the confidence of pupils and make them more ready to take risks, try new approaches, and develop a constructively critical attitude to their own work.'

Word processing is the most common use made of personal computers. It is quite straightforward to learn, and the process involved in producing documents is easy to understand. It is easy to integrate word processing use into most subject areas. In any context where pupils have to produce written work they can be asked to produce the same text in a word processed form. In these cases the text would simply be typed into the computer, stored on a disk, and printed out.

More advanced uses may be made of word processing software to create desk top publishing (DTP) products. In these cases the presentation of the text is more complex, and pictures can be included.

Supporting pupils

The use of word processing packages to prepare documents offers two major advantages for the pupil: improved presentation and provisionality.

Improved presentation can stimulate pupils to improve the quality of the document content. Seeing their own words in a neat, well-presented format can be very enjoyable for pupils who have anxieties about their handwriting. Another important benefit is automatic spelling correction. Although this is not a substitute for personal spelling skills, it can help to improve the confidence of pupils who have anxieties which interfere with their willingness to work on tasks. More advanced or older pupils can start to think about designing the presentation of documents.

Provisionality is provided by the fact that it is easy to make changes to word processed documents. This has many advantages in a classroom context. It makes it easier to encourage pupils to check, correct and redraft work, because a rewrite is much less of a chore. At a basic level this can mean removing obvious errors. Older pupils can start to think about using alternative wording, or rearranging the order of paragraphs. More advanced pupils can use this feature of word processing packages to let them prepare outlines of essays in advance, or to explore the effects of making different changes to text documents.

Supporting teaching

Teachers can make use of word processing to help them with their own work. Word processing can be used to create the documents that are used in teaching, such as handouts and worksheets. With practice this can be quicker than writing them by hand, and the quality will generally be higher. If teachers want pupils to produce high quality documentation then they must lead by example.

Teachers can also use word processing to work with pupils. For example, they can produce outline or template documents, and distribute them in electronic form to the class. If they want pupils, say, to write-up an experiment under a given set of headings they could create a document which consists just of these headings, plus empty space. Teachers can then copy this file from their disk (or over the network) to each pupil. Pupils then fill in the gaps. If teachers want to give more help than this they provide more of the text themselves, and leave smaller gaps.

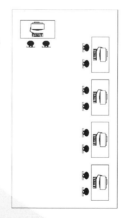

Traditional network setup

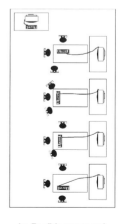

An English approach

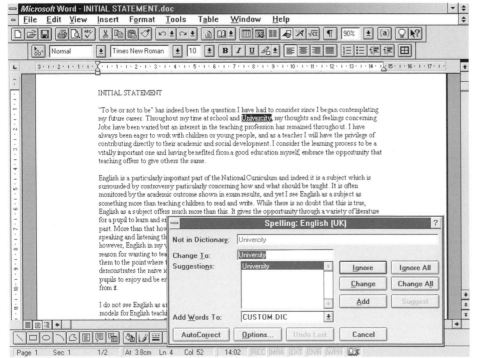

As well as typing in text a typical modern word processor offers the following key features:

Delete and insert
There is no difficulty in making changes to a word processed text. Characters and words can be altered easily and without any untidiness.

Cut and paste
Blocks of text can be cut from the document and inserted into new positions. In this way the text can be completely rearranged without the need for re-typing.

Spell check
The computer has an internal dictionary of words, and will identify any word in the pupils' text which is not found in this dictionary. A modern word processing package uses phonetics to find the nearest matches to the word, and offers these as alternative spellings. Note that the computer will not find all spelling mistakes (for example, the common their/there confusions will not be caught by a spell check).

Text formatting
The computer will allow the pupil to add emphasis, for example to headings, using bold or italic text. The pupil can also select print size and style (font). Such options should be used with reference to the purpose and audience for the document, not just for the sake of it.

Text can be arranged in columns (similar to a newspaper layout) or in tables to format particular blocks of text.

Working on tasks
The main disadvantage of producing text using word processing is that the pupil is not as free to continue the task outside of the classroom, e.g. for homework. It is important to ensure that time and resources are available for the pupils to produce any documentation which is required in word processed form.

It is better for pupils to compose the work as they type, rather than copy-type from documents they have written by hand. This can be very boring for pupils. It can put them off using the computer, and it takes away the advantage of provisionality. Ideally as pupils become confident they should be constantly revising and correcting as they work on the document. Copying an essay word-for-word removes this major advantage.

Resource requirements
Word processing does not require advanced equipment. Almost any computer/printer combination can be used to produce word processed documents, and the software is very widely available.

In some classrooms pupils have to share computers. This is not satisfactory for most word processing tasks. If pupils are using the word processor to compose new documents, as they would when working with pen and paper, then they have to have uninterrupted one-to-one access.

There are group tasks which could be carried out in pairs or groups using word processing software, such as writing letters to request information or producing a class newsletter. It is important to organise 'off-computer' work for pupils, such as task planning, preparing graphic work, etc.

Desk top publishing
Older word processing packages simply allowed you to prepare plain text documents, set out as a simple typed page. DTP packages were an exciting new development, allowing the user to create advanced effects by adding pictures and arranging text on the page like a professional printer.

Nowadays the distinction between these two types of package is less important. Modern word processing packages include many DTP features. With practice a word processing package such as *Microsoft Word* can produce almost any kind of document.

Standards

13

Trainees must demonstrate in relation to the subject and age(s) of pupils to be taught that they:

a. **know how to use ICT to find things out,** including, as appropriate for the subjects and the age of pupils to be taught:
   iv. collecting and structuring data and storing it for later retrieval, interpretation and correction;
   v. interpreting what is retrieved;

b. **know how to use ICT to try things out, make things happen and understand how they happen** as appropriate for the subject(s) and the age of pupils to be taught:
   i. exploring alternatives;
   ii. modelling relationships;
   iii. considering cause and effect;
   iv. predicting patterns and rules recognising patterns, and hypothesising.

14

Trainees must demonstrate that they know those features of ICT which can be used, separately or together, to support teaching and learning in subjects, including:

a. **speed and automatic functions** - the function of ICT which enables routine tasks to be completed and repeated quickly, allowing the user to concentrate on thinking and on tasks such as analysing and looking for patterns within data, asking questions and looking for answers, and explaining and presenting results.

c. **provisionality** - the function of ICT which allows changes to be made easily and enables alternatives to be explored readily, and as appropriate to the subject(s) and age of pupils to be taught:
   i. how to make best use of the ability to make rapid changes, including how to create text, designs and models which may be explored and improved in the light of evaluation; e.g. spreadsheet models;

d. **interactivity -** the function of ICT which enables rapid and dynamic feedback and response, as appropriate to the subject(s) and age of pupils to be taught, including how to determine the most appropriate media to use,.e.g. the changing values in a spreadsheet.

A spreadsheet is a grid of cells in which values can be laid out and calculations performed. Spreadsheets can be used effectively in the classroom whenever calculations must be performed. Spreadsheets are an example of 'modelling' software, i.e. programs which simulate a real or possible event in order to observe, test or predict its behaviour.

Spreadsheets have several advantages over a pocket calculator:

- Interactive – one big advantage is that once a set of formulas have been added to a spreadsheet you can vary the initial values as often as you like, and observe the changes in results.

- Checkable – the calculation and the values are set out on the screen, so they are easy to check and print out. As a teacher you can check exactly what work the pupil has done, and locate the source of any errors. Older pupils can use this facility to check their own work.

- Variety of output – the pupil can print out the completed spreadsheet. It is also very easy to generate and print out graphs from the values shown in the spreadsheet.

The theoretical basis of spreadsheet use is the concept of modelling but a teacher can make good use of spreadsheet software in the classroom without discussing the concept of modelling at all.

Supporting pupils

In any classroom activity where calculations are required a spreadsheet may be used as a learning tool. The same considerations apply to the use of a spreadsheet to perform calculations as apply to the use of calculators. That is, both items can be useful tools, but the decision to use them should be taken with care. As a general rule calculators and spreadsheets are not appropriate where the purpose of the lesson is to develop and practise calculation skills. However in many cases the performance of calculations is secondary to the lesson objective. In these cases it may be very appropriate to use ICT to simplify the task, so the pupils can concentrate on the real purpose of the lesson.

Spreadsheets also have an important place in Mathematics lessons. They can be used to check calculations, for example, or to demonstrate how the structure of a formula affects the resulting value.

There are two very different ways in which spreadsheets can be used:

- The pupils can make use of a spreadsheet model that has been created for them by the teacher.

- The pupils can create a new spreadsheet from scratch, devising the layout and creating the formulas.

The former use is much simpler for the pupil. It is particularly appropriate where the spreadsheet is of secondary importance, and the pupils are primarily interested in the results of the calculation rather than how they are derived.

Spreadsheets may be used to give pupils speedy access to the results of calculations. This can be of value either to check their own work, or to use calculated values to support other objectives, for example in science or economics. Spreadsheets can also be used simply to present results, for example if pupils have been collecting the results of a survey, they can enter the totals into a spreadsheet, and generate a graph.

Supporting teaching

Teachers can share the task of creating a spreadsheet with their pupils. They can create the structure of the spreadsheet, entering the arithmetic formulas needed to derive the results, but leaving space for the data values. A copy of the spreadsheet is then given to the pupils, either on a disk or over the network, who can collect and enter values, and observe the results.

Modelling

A mathematical model uses formulas to simulate the results of an event. A set of values represents starting conditions, and then mathematical rules are applied to those original values, and a result is obtained. The original values can be divided into 'variables' which can be altered, and 'constants' which cannot be altered. The result of the calculation is sometimes called the 'derived' value.

Models can relate to very simple events. For example, entering into a spreadsheet the amount of money available to spend on a shopping trip and the values of the items to be purchased, adding up the total cost of the items and subtracting this from the amount of money available will show if everything is affordable. In this model:

- the constant is the amount of money available (because this is fixed)
- the variables are the costs of the items to be purchased (because they could change buying plans)
- the mathematical rules are 'add together the costs of the items' and 'subtract costs from the spending money'
- the derived value is the amount of money left over after purchases.

This model could be used to test the combination of items that could be purchased. It can also be used in another way. The variables can be altered in order to answer new queries, for example, what if a less expensive pair of jeans were purchased? This use of models is known as a 'What if...' query.

In real life this kind of task can be achieved using mental arithmetic while shopping, though it could be set out in a spreadsheet. Spreadsheets can create highly complex models, using large numbers of variables, or very complicated mathematical rules. It is possible to purchase ready-made models, for example, a file which models the movement of planets round the Sun, or the growth of the population over time.

Most computer games are complex models which take the values which the player enters (such as the speed and angle of a shot) and present results (such as whether the target has been hit or not). In this case the variables are set by a motion sensor such as a joystick, and the results are displayed in the form of on-screen graphics.

Spreadsheet software offers the following key features:

Arithmetic functions

The spreadsheet allows you to set out mathematical formulas using the normal operators ($+ - * /$) and a wide range of functions (such as Sum, Average, Cosines, etc.) Many mathematical operations which the pupil has learned can be copied on the spreadsheet.

Layout and formatting

The words and numbers in a spreadsheet can be formatted in the same way as in a word processed document, to improve the appearance of the final product.

Graphs

Most modern spreadsheet packages have a graph function. Selecting a set of numbers from the spreadsheet and the computer uses these to create a graph of the form you choose (line, bar, pie, etc.)

'IF'

More advanced pupils may want to make use of the IF function. This allows you to vary the results shown in a spreadsheet. For example, IF a negative value is entered THEN display a warning message.

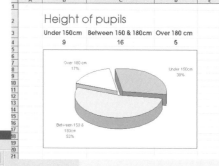

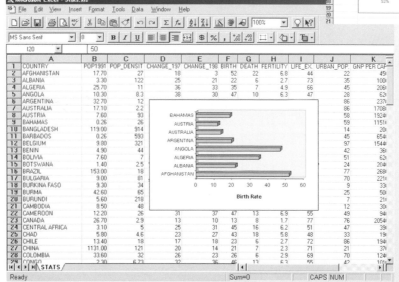

Standards

13

Trainees must demonstrate in relation to the subject and age(s) of pupils to be taught that they:

a. know how to use ICT to find things out, including, as appropriate for the subjects and the age of pupils to be taught:
   i. identifying sources of information and discriminating between them;
   ii. planning and putting together a search strategy, including framing useful questions, widening and narrowing down searches;
   iii. how to search for information, including using key words and strings and logical operators such as AND, OR and NOT, indexes and directories;
   iv. collecting and structuring data and storing it for later retrieval, interpretation and correction;
   v. interpreting what is retrieved;
   vi. considering validity, reliability and reasonableness of outcomes;

d. interactivity - the function of ICT which enables rapid and dynamic feedback and response, as appropriate to the subject(s) and age of pupils to be taught, including how to determine the most appropriate media to use, e.g. the responses to queries of an Internet search engine.

17

Trainees must demonstrate that they know how each of the following is relevant to the specialist subject and phase for which they are training:

b. reference resources, including;
   i. how to search reference resources;
   ii. how to incorporate the use of reference resources into teaching; e.g. reference CD-ROMs and World Wide Web sites on the Internet.

A database enables a large body of information to be stored in a structured form for ease of retrieval. In this section traditional database software is discussed, together with the less structured methods which are now available for searching for information.

Unlike word processing and spreadsheet packages, there is no common standard database package which is widely used. There are fewer reasons for the occasional user to work with a database package. Modern data search techniques have developed over the past decade to make it easier for the casual user to search large bodies of unstructured information. This has meant that there is less need to make use of specialist database handling techniques.

Informal searches

Informal methods of information retrieval are of increasing importance nowadays, and are probably more useful in the classroom than formal database searches. The two main sources of useful information for pupils and teachers are CD-ROMs and the World Wide Web.

Different CD-ROMs offer different techniques for locating useful contents. They may have indexes or contents pages like a book, and they may allow key word or subject searches. To find information on the World Wide Web use a search engine. There are a variety of these with slightly different methods, but they basically allow key word searches. The key words may be combined to create complex search criteria.

Supporting your pupils

The least satisfactory use of database software in the classroom is to expect pupils individually to create a database from scratch, store information in it, and then use search techniques to locate the data they have entered. Creating a database structure is a fairly advanced skill, and is probably out of place except in specialist IT lessons. Collecting and adding information is time-consuming to construct a worthwhile database.

A more useful technique would be for the teacher to establish a central database, and get the class to collect and add information. For example, after a field trip or a series of classroom experiments, pupils could pool their findings into a single common database. In most cases, however, informal search techniques will be more useful to pupils.

Supporting your teaching

Many teachers use spreadsheet software to set up a database structure and accumulate a table of data. This has several advantages. Firstly, pupils may already be familiar with the use of spreadsheets. Secondly, a spreadsheet table presents all of the information as a simple 'flat file' table. The pupils can easily see the extent and contents of the database simply by looking at the screen.

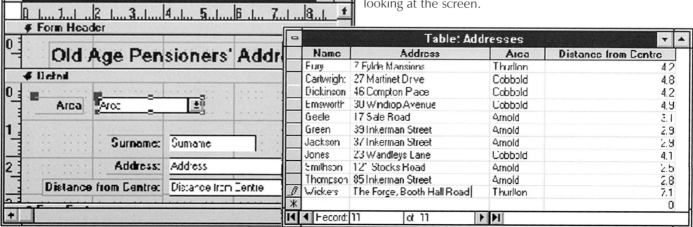

Database structures

All conventional databases share the same basic structure. All the information about a single person or thing is stored in a *record*. Each record is divided into *fields*. Each field stores a single 'fact' about the person or thing that is the subject of the record. Every record in the database contains the same fields, in the same order. In other words the database is a bit like an old-fashioned card file. The records are like the cards in the file, and the fields are like the pieces of information written on the card.

When a database is printed out it is conventionally arranged as a table. Each record takes up a single row of the table, and each field takes up a single column. Spreadsheet software can be used to create a database table. Spreadsheets usually include database commands such as sorting or searching through the table of data.

Complex searches

A normal search is carried out by entering a word. The computer finds records that contain this word. The word match which you specify is known as the *Search Criteria*. For example when searching a database of pupils you could enter search criteria such as:

SURNAME = 'Hughes'

Where a field contains a numerical value it is often possible to specify a search using relational operators (such as < meaning 'less than'). A complex search can contain more than one search criterion. For example:

SURNAME = 'Hughes' AND AGE < 7

In this case the two criteria are combined using the logical operator AND.

Modern search engines allow you to specify less formal search criteria, but it is still possible to combine more than one criterion in order to narrow down the search.

Administration and data protection

In some cases schools have sophisticated administrative database systems established. It is useful to be aware of the type of data available, e.g. class lists, exam results, etc. Some teachers make personal use of a database to help with administrative tasks in school. A computer file equivalent to paper-based class records will give rapid access to data and make analysis simple. However, teachers must be aware of the implications of the Data Protection Act.

The key tasks which can be performed with a database are:

Search

This is the main information handling skill that your pupils will find useful. Different software packages offer different ways of carrying out a search but the main technique is to find matches to the words which the pupil enters. Searches can be simple or complex.

Edit

In some cases you may wish the pupils to make changes to the information stored in a database. This can include adding or deleting records, or making amendments to the information in a record.

Output

It is generally possible to display on the screen a single record, a selection of records, or the entire database.

Sort

If a database is sorted it can be displayed or printed out in a particular order: alphabetical, chronological or numerical. You normally have to specify which order to use (e.g. a library database can be sorted in order of book title, subject or author). In some cases sorting permanently rearranges a database. In other cases the records return to their original order after they have been printed out.

Using ICT

Articles in Book Citation

Author:	Capel, S, Leask, M, Turner, T.
Publication Year:	(1995)
Article Title:	
Editor:	
Book Title:	Learning to Teach in the Secondary School
Edition:	
Place of publication:	London
Publisher:	Routledge
Page Numbers:	
Shelf Reference:	
Key words:	school experiance, classroom management, pupil differences.
Notes:	A must for the PGCE course, it covers everything from the student teacher's role to getting a job.

Citation Database Main Menu

Add / View / Delete Records

Articles in Book

Search Citation Database

Print Citation Database

Export Citation Database

Quit Citation Database

Using graphics software

Standards

14

Trainees must demonstrate that they know those features of ICT which can be used, separately or together, to support teaching and learning in subjects, including:

b. **capacity and range** - the function of ICT, as appropriate to the subject(s) and age of pupils to be taught, to access and to handle large amounts of information; change timescales, or remove barriers of distance; give teachers and pupils access to and control over situations which would normally be outside their everyday experience, including:

   i. the range of forms in which ICT can present information;

c. **provisionality** - the function of ICT which allows changes to be made easily and enables alternatives to be explored readily, and as appropriate to the subject(s) and age of pupils to be taught:

   i. how to make best use of the ability to make rapid changes, including how to create text, designs and models which may be explored and improved in the light of evaluation;

   ii. how to judge when and when not to encourage exploration and change using ICT;

   iii. how saving work at different stages enables a record to be kept of the development of ideas, e.g, computer aided design and manufacture.

Graphics software packages are generally enjoyable to learn and use. It is not usually difficult to encourage pupils to make use of graphics software in the classroom: the difficulty can be in trying to ensure that they use it in a focused and productive way.

Most graphics packages offer a range of drawing and painting 'tools' and a palette of colours. The tools and colours are selected and manipulated using the mouse.

Supporting your pupils

The main issue when incorporating graphics software into a lesson is to keep pupils' attention focused on the task in hand. To ensure that a graphics task is properly focused pupils need to be encouraged to reflect on their work. Discuss the purpose of the task in advance, and pause to review the work in progress. Graphics software makes it easy to revise the images that your pupils create. You can take advantage of this feature to encourage them to check, correct and improve their work.

More advanced pupils should be taught how to paste graphics into a text document. This will improve the quality and usefulness of the final outcome, and it emphasises the fact that the graphics must perform a function within a context. All pupils can enhance documents by looking through collections of clip art and selecting appropriate images to paste into the text.

Using graphics software in subject lessons can enhance pupils' learning in a number of ways:

Improved presentation

It is often important to incorporate the production of some kind of image or graphic into a task, but many pupils lack confidence in their drawing ability. As with the effect of word processing on text, graphics software can increase pupils' confidence and stimulate them to improve the content of their work, by giving them access to improved presentation.

Ease of editing

Because it is much easier to make changes to a graphic when it is prepared on the computer, pupils can be encouraged to evaluate and revise their own work. More advanced pupils can explore the effects of making various changes.

Enhancing text

Pupils can start to use graphics as a supplement to text, selecting between the two modes of presentation as appropriate. Images and texts can be combined together into single documents.

Easter Island

Coursework Project

Supporting your teaching

You should aim to become confident enough to prepare any graphics that you need to include in your teaching materials using computer software.

Resource requirements

The main disadvantage of graphics software is that it can be demanding of resources, particularly in relation to memory capacity and printing.

Storage

Graphics files take up a great deal of memory space. A single graphics file can take up most of the space on a floppy disk. This may be a good opportunity to teach pupils how to check a disk for storage capacity and to be ruthless in deleting multiple versions of graphics files. In any case teachers and pupils should be aware of storage requirements, and plan a strategy to ensure that there is space available to store the work which has been created.

Printing

If pupils want to print out their multi-coloured designs the teacher will need to ensure access to colour printers. There may be a limited number of colour printers available for pupils to use. Teachers also need to be aware of the length of time it can take to print out a single coloured graphic: in a large class pupils may have to be sent one at a time over several lessons to complete the printing task. If the final piece has been created in colour but is to be printed out in black and white a trial print will need to be done to see how the colours translate.

Clip art and photographs

Ready-made graphics files are available on almost any subject. These pictures are known as 'clip art', and are available from CD-ROMs and the Internet. Some graphics are copyright-free, some you can buy and use in any context, and some need to be specially licensed. There is a lot of free clip art on the Internet, and you can buy packs of CD-ROMs with literally thousands of pictures on them very cheaply.

Giving pupils access to clip art is a good way of enhancing their work, and giving them design control. It is, however, important for pupils to assess the quality and appropriateness of the images, and to consider carefully the size of each image, and the number to be used.

Ready-made photographs are also available on CD-ROMs. Depending on the quality required, the file size of an individual image can be larger than the capacity of a single floppy disk. Original photographs can be scanned in directly. Special software is available to manipulate the photograph.

Graphics software offers the following key features:

Shapes and lines

The simplest items to draw are shapes and lines. Creating pictures with these elements is a good way to introduce pupils to the use of the mouse.

Texts

To produce useful graphics it is often necessary to add text, as a caption, label or design element. Text may be formatted for style, size and colour. More advanced graphics packages include tools for applying special effects to text, such as depth, texture, shadow, etc.

Select

Depending on the type of package in use it is possible to select either an area of the screen or one of the elements which make up the design. This element can be cut, copied and pasted within the graphic.

Resize and stretch

Selected elements can be stretched and reshaped.

Bitmap or vector?

There are two main types of graphics package. These create and store pictures in different ways.

Bitmap packages store pictures by storing the position and colour of every dot in the picture. Vector packages on the other hand store the angle and length of every line that makes up the picture. This gives a quite different feel to the two types of package, and has an effect on the type of activity you are able to perform..

Many basic software packages, in particular those with the word 'Paint' in the title, are bitmap packages. Packages with the word 'Draw' in the title tend to be vector-based, as are the built-in graphics functions that are available with many modern word processing packages.

A graphics tablet can be used instead of a mouse to draw 'on screen'

Standards

13

Trainees must demonstrate in relation to the subject and age(s) of pupils to be taught that they:

c. **know how to use ICT to communicate and exchange ideas** as appropriate for the subjects and the age of pupils to be taught:

  i. presenting ideas, including: identification of audience and purpose; deciding the best means with which to communicate;

  ii. exchanging ideas, including identifying the most appropriate medium, and information

14

Trainees must demonstrate that they know those features of ICT which can be used, separately or together, to support teaching and learning in subjects, including:

d. **Interactivity** - the function of ICT which enables rapid and dynamic feedback and response, as appropriate to the subject(s) and age of pupils to be taught, including how to determine the most appropriate media to use.

Multimedia provides an exciting new way of presenting information in an interactive and non-linear format. Web page design now incorporates multimedia features. Many primary school children are already developing skills in using multimedia authoring packages. This important capability needs to be extended in the secondary school.

What is multimedia?

Multimedia is the mixing of different forms of media within one program. Such media may include text, graphics – in the form of drawings, clip art, scanned photographs or images from digital cameras – video clips, sound clips or animations. Multimedia is not the same as 'multiple-media', which is the use of different forms of media, e.g. printed materials, video-cassettes and flip-charts (and possibly computers) in a presentation of information.

A vast array of commercial multimedia programs are currently available which attempt to stimulate and intrigue pupils through the use of a range of computer-generated media. These range from the popular talking books, designed to engage early readers through to complex CD-ROM based reference material. The key to the success of each is often in its level of interactivity, i.e. the way in which the user can, to a greater or lesser extent, determine the order in which the various elements are presented.

Multimedia authoring

Special software, called 'multimedia authoring' packages, are now sufficiently straightforward and robust for pupils to use. They provide opportunities for pupils not just to respond to commercial multimedia programs but also to be able to design and author their own multimedia material for others to use.

These packages are underpinned by their ability to create and link a series of computer 'screens' which can be linked dynamically through the creation of buttons or 'hotspots'. By clicking on these the user can navigate to another screen, reveal text, hear a sound or play an animation or video. Many packages now have the facility to create buttons which activate Web links, opening up the possibility of pupils publishing material directly linked to the Internet.

What are pupils learning?

Apart from developing a range of key ICT skills, the use of multimedia authoring packages allows pupils to:

- communicate ideas which would be difficult if only text were used
- examine the needs of a target audience
- engage in a real design process
- critically evaluate their product
- develop skills of negotiation and collaboration in, and use ICT to support, learning across a range of curriculum areas.

Pupils could create their own talking storybook, a school guide for new pupils or visiting parents, a language-matching exercise, a history quiz – the possibilities are limitless.

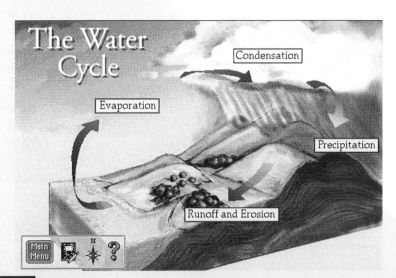

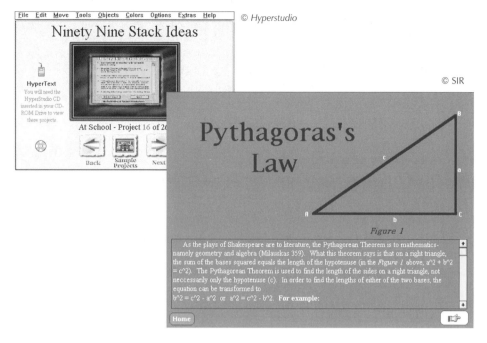

© Hyperstudio

© SIR

Classroom management

Multimedia authoring with pupils takes time and the files which are created, particularly those using graphics and sound, take up lots of disk space. This can be controlled to some extent by encouraging pupils to create small, successful presentations rather than undertaking a complicated but ultimately unfinished and frustrating project. Collaborative team-work and undertaking preparation away from the computers are important considerations which should be thought about during the initial planning process. The activity seems to be more successful when groups contain different pupils, each with a specific skill and function, with roles being rotated systematically. Successful multimedia authoring requires pupils to spend a great deal of time designing on paper, gathering and creating content and finally working with the computers.

The hardware and software

Effective work with multimedia authoring requires access to modern computer hardware which includes a sound card and a CD-ROM drive. A scanner and digital camera are also recommended.

Presentation packages such as *PowerPoint* can be used to author multimedia materials, but they can only produce linear presentations. One of the most popular packages used in primary schools is *Hyperstudio*. It allows the user to:

- add graphics, either from other paint packages or more simply with built in paint tools
- to import pictures from clip art, cameras, scanners or photo CD-ROMs
- to type in text
- to add sound or video clips
- and finally to link these together through the creation of hotspots or buttons.

In practice

Many pupils now arrive in Year 7 having had some previous experience of using a program like *Hyperstudio*. The potential of multimedia authoring has been slow to develop in secondary schools, however, and many of pupils' skills become redundant. *Hyperstudio* could certainly be used widely with Key Stage 3 pupils, with Year 10 and 11 pupils moving on to simple Web-based authoring packages, and for the most able and interested, the more sophisticated professional multimedia authoring packages.

Multimedia software often uses the following terms:

Navigation

On certain screens the user is given a number of options as which part of the program to move to next. It is usual to include 'back' and 'home' keys to prevent the user from getting 'lost' in the program.

Hotspots

It is possible to create areas of the screen where, if the mouse is clicked on, something will happen. This might be as obvious as a graphic of a button, or it could be a key word or an image. Further text, a photo, animation or video might appear, or it might take the user to a different screen.

Storyboard

Multimedia sequences are difficult to conceive. They need to be planned first on paper using conventional film 'storyboard' techniques. Unlike those used in films, however, these will need to include multi-pathways or 'branches'.

Cast members

This refers to the list of text boxes, drawings, photographs, video-clips and sounds that will be drawn together in the program. Each member needs to be prepared and named separately, ready to be called up when needed.

Multimedia on the Internet

World Wide Web pages on the Internet are examples of multimedia software. Through the use of hypertext (hotspot) links pages can deliver text, images, sound music and video. Authoring languages such as HTML (hypertext mark-up language) are relatively simple to master. Languages such as Java offer greater scope but are more difficult.

Standards

13

Trainees must demonstrate in relation to the subject and age(s) of pupils to be taught that they:

a. know how to use ICT to find things out, including, as appropriate for the subjects and the age of pupils to be taught:
   i. identifying sources of information and discriminating between them;
   ii. planning and putting together a search strategy, including framing useful questions, widening and narrowing down searches;
   iii. how to search for information, including using key words and strings and logical operators such as AND, OR and NOT, indexes and directories;
   vi. collecting and structuring data and storing it for later retrieval, interpretation and correction;
   v. interpreting what is retrieved;
   vi. considering validity, reliability and reasonableness of outcomes;

b. capacity and range - the function of ICT, as appropriate to the subject(s) and age of pupils to be taught, to access and to handle large amounts of information; change timescales, or remove barriers of distance; give teachers and pupils access to and control over situations which would normally be outside their everyday experience, including:
   i. the range of forms in which ICT can present information;
   ii. the range of possible appropriate ICT sources, including local sources such as CD-ROM, and remote databases such as the Internet and the National Grid for Learning;
   iii. how to judge the accuracy of the information and the credibility of its source;
   iv. how ICT can be used to gain access to expertise outside the classroom, the school and the local community through communications with experts.

d. interactivity - the function of ICT which enables rapid and dynamic feedback and response, as appropriate to the subject(s) and age of pupils to be taught, including how to determine the most appropriate media to use, e.g. the responses to queries of an Internet search engine.

17

Trainees must demonstrate that they know how each of the following is relevant to the specialist subject and phase for which they are training:

b. reference resources, including;
   i. how to search reference resources;
   ii. how to incorporate the use of reference resources into teaching.

There are good educational reasons for using the Internet, such as undertaking research, obtaining up-to-date news and weather reports, sending and receiving E-mail, using chatlines, using forums and publishing Web pages.

The Internet started as a defence-related network. It has grown into a global network of linked computer networks making a ' Web' of connections. The Web now contains many thousands of 'sites' linking millions of contributors and users.

Using the facilities of the Internet it is possible for teachers and pupils to:

* access information on almost any subject
* learn and revise using multimedia teaching and learning materials
* distribute and contribute to research using on-line questionnaires
* download software and data files
* order resources
* browse library catalogues around the world
* obtain up-to-date news and weather reports
* send and receive E-mail
* communicate with people having similar interests using chatlines and forums
* publish information for others to see.

Web pages

Information on the WWW is organised into 'pages', each one with its own unique address on the network called a URL (uniform resource locator). The pages are accessed using this address which appears in the 'location' box of the Web browser. The address is typed in or can be automatically entered from the 'bookmark' or 'favourite' function of the browser. 'Bookmarking' enables the address of sites to be stored avoiding the necessity for 'browsing' to get to them.

On a Web page text, pictures and graphics can be 'hot-linked' to other pages. The links are usually referred to as hypertext links. Jumping from one link to another is called 'browsing'

Pages are created using a programming language, the most commonly used is HTML (hypertext mark-up language). Authoring can be done using a word processor or a special authoring package. Most schools will have their own Web site by the millennium. Teachers and pupils will increasingly be contributors to the resources of the WWW. A school can also gain valuable publicity by having its own Web site!

Using Web sites to support learning

Research

It is often said that any book containing information is out-of-date as soon as it is published, and the Internet can help overcome this problem. However, information on the Internet often has less rigour and control over its content than paper-based publications. Anyone can publish information on the Internet, regardless of how little they know about a subject and who they represent. Pupils have to learn to be discerning, selective authors to use the resources effectively.

Before letting a class loose on the Internet teachers need a strategy that will identify promising material and avoids the more dubious Web sites. In particular, look for sites that provide useful hot links to other sites. Pupils enjoy surfing productively, but they go off-task quickly if they cannot find relevant information.

Browsing

Learning to use a browser teaches pupils useful search skills. Give some basic starting points (how to type in Internet addresses or URLs and use the 'back' and 'forward' buttons), but let them make their own mistakes. Encourage pupils to keep the addresses of useful Web sites for their future use. Using a search engine teaches pupils important research techniques. The key to success is learning how to define and refine searches to find exactly what is required.

Bookmarks

Teachers need to build up a personal list of useful Web sites, and amend this as necessary. Bookmarks can be kept on a disk and imported into the browser. Provide pupils with a list of bookmarks to work from or put the topic links onto a school Web site page for pupils to download.

Creating learning material using Web resources

Text and images are easily saved to file and can provide invaluable resources for a teacher to engineer worksheets and other classroom resources. Running a word processor in the background behind the browser and cut and paste information from Web pages into it. A single Word file can then be compiled which can be stored, adapted and printed at an appropriate time. Most school systems will probably control what can be downloaded from the Internet, both because of the danger of offensive material ending up on the system, and of computer viruses. Students can be shown how to author resources in a similar way. There are ethical and legal issues associated with using other people intellectual property and pupils need to be aware of these.

Teachers can author pages for their classes or to teach core skills across the school. Pages can set tasks and support them with WWW resources provided as hypertext links. Schools are rapidly constructing a network of resources, produced internally, aimed at supporting aspects of learning across the curriculum. Pages aimed predominantly at the people within an organisation are often termed an 'Intranet'. Intranet pages can be reserved for internal use only, which may give more scope for creativity on the part of pupils and teachers without the need for rigorous authoring that needs to be done before Internet pages go on-line.

Designing Web pages

The design of Web pages is a skill that teachers and pupils can learn quite easily. It provides scope for providing structured learning experiences for a class or for pupils to exercise their creative abilities and ability to structure information. Material can be linked into non-linear sequences which can support open-learning of the type that other multimedia resources offer. Ideally teachers need to develop a basic grasp of an appropriate authoring language, such as HTML, to be able to support pupils. However, the latest versions of applications such as Microsoft *Office '98* provide the option to save the file as a Web document. Pupils can be highly motivated by seeing their word processor files published on the Internet.

Chat-lines, forums, newsgroups and mailbases

The Internet is as much about people communicating with other people as it is a network of hardware links. Groups of people sharing a common interest is a powerful way of learning. Pupils may find these resources useful when researching a topic, but pupils need to be warned about releasing personal information. Not all interests are of academic value and pupils will gravitate to chat about soap operas, pop stars and football. Ensure that pupils are not using 'chat' during a lesson without permission: a skilled computer user can move quickly between screens when a teacher approaches!

WWW or Internet?

The World Wide Web(WWW)is a particular set of resources on the Internet. It contains 'pages' of information which are accessed by using the mouse to 'point and click' on words or pictures (often known as 'browsing'). These hypertext links connect to further pages of information which may contain, sound and music files, pictures, video and animations.

To view pages on the WWW users need a graphical 'browser' such as Netscape or Microsoft's Internet Explorer.

Staying on task

Supervise what pupils are doing while they are on-line. Given the chance, many will gravitate towards chat lines or Web sites related to pop singers and films.

If the school system does not have a filtering facility that prevents the downloading of offensive material you will have to be vigilant during lessons.

Printing out

Pupils tend to print whole Web pages which contain only small amounts of useful information, because this is easy to do. They should be taught to be selective and to copy relevant material to a word processing file.

Graphics that look good on the screen may not look so good when printed in black and white. Using a colour printer could prove to be expensive. It may be best to discourage the printing of graphics unless they are essential.

Things to do

- Download an HTML tutorial and learn how to produce WWW pages of your own. For the location of a tutorial see: http://www.cant.ac.uk/title
- Access the Government's National Grid for Learning at: http://www.ngfl.gov.uk
- Try the Virtual Teachers' Centre at: http://www.vtc.ngfl.gov.uk

Further information

The benefits of ICT in subject teaching
Finding things out
Legal and ethical issues
The professional use of ICT
Key sources of information

Standards

13

Trainees must demonstrate in relation to the subject and age(s) of pupils to be taught that they:

c. know how to use ICT to communicate and exchange ideas as appropriate to the subject(s) and the age of pupils to be taught:
   i. presenting ideas, including: identification of audience and purpose; deciding the best means with which to communicate;
   ii. exchanging ideas, including identifying the most appropriate medium, and information.

14

Trainees must demonstrate that they know those features of ICT which can be used, separately or together, to support teaching and learning in subjects, including:

b. **capacity and range** - the function of ICT, as appropriate to the subject(s) and age of pupils to be taught, to access and to handle large amounts of information; change timescales, or remove barriers of distance; give teachers and pupils access to and control over situations which would normally be outside their everyday experience, including:
   i. the range of forms in which ICT can present information;

d. **interactivity** - the function of ICT which enables rapid and dynamic feedback and response, as appropriate to the subject(s) and age of pupils to be taught, including how to determine the most appropriate media to use.

> *'Try a link-up with a fellow student teacher's class!'*

Writing for a purpose, and for a different audience, is very important for a pupil. The thought that another person, perhaps thousands of miles away, can be sent an electronic 'letter' which can be received in less than a minute is a very powerful experience for most people.

The 'National Grid for Learning' initiative is going to connect all schools to the Internet. Once a school has the necessary E-mail facilities the next stage is to try to set up some links with other local, national and international schools.

● ●

E-mail messages travel via an 'electronic post office', where they wait until the intended recipient checks if there are any messages. Each user has a unique identification code (i.e. an address) which ensures that users get only the messages intended for them. Not all schools will be able to manage to provide an E-mail address for each pupil: they may have to share.

Managing E-mail

In school, teachers have found that managing E-mails can be like trying to steer an avalanche! Harnessing the natural exuberance of pupils can quickly become a problem, especially when replies start to come back to the classroom. The more letters the pupils write, the more replies they receive, which leads to a greater demand for computer time. This can conflict with other uses of the computer in the school. If there is a printer attached to the computer, printouts can help with drafting replies if computer time is limited.

On-line time costs money, so teach pupils to type messages in *Word* before going on-line, store the text and then 'paste' them into the mail program.

E-mail can be a valuable tool for allowing pupils to communicate with the world at large; it can also be abused, with inappropriate materials being both sent and received. The school's Internet provider will supply the school with at least one E-mail address, but pupils may have been allocated their own addresses already. If there is only one address, how will pupils identify themselves so that messages reach the right person in the school?

It is important to ensure the pupils follow 'classroom rules' for the use of E-mails. It will probably be necessary to ration the use of the computer for E-mails, perhaps limited to one session a week. If you have a 'partner' school, inform them that you are limited in time and access to hardware. Whatever system is used it is very important that it is fair and ensures that all pupils have equal access.

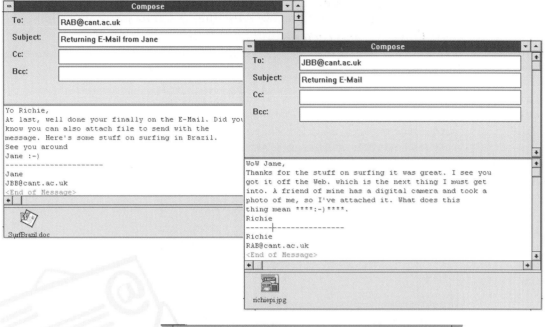

Email windows:

To: RAB@cant.ac.uk
Subject: Returning E-Mail from Jane
Cc:
Bcc:

```
Yo Richie,
At last, well done your finally on the E-Mail. Did you
know you can also attach file to send with the
message. Here's some stuff on surfing in Brazil.
See you around
Jane :-)
----------------------
Jane
JBB@cant.ac.uk
<End of Message>
```
SurfBrazil.doc

To: JBB@cant.ac.uk
Subject: Returning E-Mail
Cc:
Bcc:

```
WoW Jane,
Thanks for the stuff on surfing it was great. I see you
got it off the Web. which is the next thing I must get
into. A friend of mine has a digital camera and took a
photo of me, so I've attached it. What does this
thing mean ****:-)****.
Richie
-----+----------------
Richie
RAB@cant.ac.uk
<End of Message>
```
richiepi.jpg

To: RAB@cant.ac.uk
Subject:
Cc:
Bcc:

```
Richie,
Thanks for the photo your looking great, what a tan it
must be all that surfing dood. As for the ":-)" its a
smiley face if you look at it from the side see
if you can work these out ... ":-(" "%-?"
Jane:-*
----------------------
Jane
JBB@cant.ac.uk
<End of Message>
```

To: JBB@cant.ac.uk
Subject: Message from Richie :-*
Cc:
Bcc:

```
Hi Jane,
thanks for the last message you sent. I think I get it now
with the faces, here's a couple I've thought of myself :-X
   :-$    ~:-O    !-)
keep in touch!
Richie
----------------------
Richard
RAB@cant.ac.uk
<End of Message>
```

When using E-mail...

- How can the teacher keep track of how many E-mails pupils are sending?
- How will the teacher ensure that the pupils have a similar entitlement for each session? What limits will be imposed (e.g. 'two paragraphs maximum')?
- How will what is typed be monitored?
- Who will have the responsibility for sending the E-mail by dialling out?
- Is the password permanently stored in the computer?
- Can pupils keep copies of their E-mails, either by storing them on the hard drive/floppy disk or printing them out?
- How can higher order language skills be encouraged, rather than simply 'Hello, I am Jim. I live at....'?

Security matters!

The teacher should make sure that:

- pupils do not include their age, home address or a telephone number in an E-mail
- the school fax or telephone number is only quoted in exceptional circumstances
- permission is obtained from parents before a photograph of the pupil is attached to an E-mail.

Things to do

- make contact with another school
- set up a mailing group with some colleagues to exchange ideas
- learn how to 'attach' files such as word processing documents.

Standards

13

Trainees must demonstrate in relation to the subject and age(s) of pupils to be taught that they:

c. **know how to use ICT to communicate and exchange ideas** as appropriate to the subject(s) and the age of pupils to be taught:

   i. presenting ideas, including: identification of audience and purpose; deciding the best means with which to communicate;

   ii. exchanging ideas, including identifying the most appropriate medium, and information.

The inclusion of the 'C' in ICT serves to re-inforce the importance of 'communication'. What we call Information Technology is not just about information, it's about how the information is communicated.

Until recently the methods of communication available to most people (beyond direct speech) were limited to letter-writing and the telephone. Other media, such as printed materials or TV images, were only created by specialists, using expensive equipment. Today we have potential access to a wide range of communications technologies such as video and digital photography (sometimes called 'lens-based media'), video-conferencing, satellite systems, etc. Increasingly all these technologies are manipulated and controlled through computer software systems. Unlike other media, once a text, graphic or sound has been digitised, manipulating and copying it does not reduce the quality of the original, and once on a computer network, can be potentially accessed by anyone across the world in a matter of minutes.

Sophisticated communication skills are becoming an essential part of everyday life, and not something that can be left to the English department to teach! All teachers of all subjects have a potential contribution to make, both in their expectations of the quality of communication skills pupils develop and in their own use of electronic media to present information to them.

In practice

At the simplest level, teachers will need to encourage pupils to use ICT to combine different forms of communication appropriately, such as using text and images in a word processing package to create a map to show where they live. This can then be extended to include a wider range of packages to produce posters, simple leaflets and short reports which use computer-generated graphs and charts. Ultimately this should lead to the production of more complex products, such as interactive multimedia presentations in which sounds, images and texts are combined together, and template-based solutions which allow others to create their own content quickly and easily.

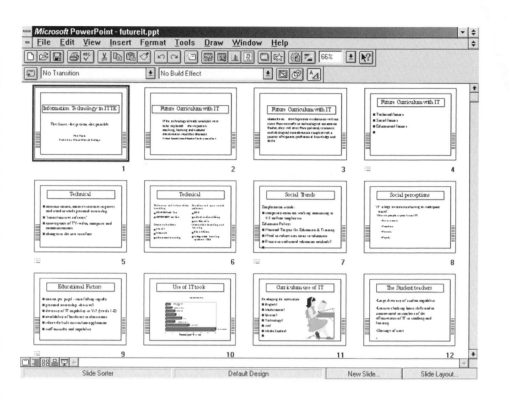

Purpose and audience

Underlying the idea of communicating information is the need to consider purpose and audience. Thinking about purpose demands that pupils define both the information that needs to be communicated and consider the impression the information needs to make. For example, a children's party invitation must include details of the date, time and place, but it must also look fun and inviting. In clarifying the purpose, the intended audience also needs to be kept in mind: a children's party invitation needs to communicate information to the parent as much as the child. These elements will influence conscious decisions about layout, typefaces, graphics, colours, etc. Analysing and evaluating existing examples of successful, and unsuccessful, communication products significantly enhances their understanding of the issues involved.

To begin with pupils are likely to be producing materials to communicate familiar ideas to familiar audiences. As they progress, however, they will need to research into areas of more unfamiliar content and into the needs of unfamiliar audiences. Ultimately they might produce single products which cater for the needs of a variety of different audiences. Pupils should be encouraged to make their own decisions about the media used, e.g. between a *PowerPoint* type presentation, a video or a Web page. This will involve evaluating the advantages and disadvantages of each, both from the point of view of the appropriateness for the content and the audience, but also in terms of the time and cost involved in their production.

What should a teacher know?

Can the teacher:

* use a wide range of electronic methods of manipulating and communicating information with confidence?
* judge the particular advantages and disadvantages of each media, including production time and cost?

Standards

17

Trainees must demonstrate that they know how each of the following is relevant to the specialist subject and phase for which they are training:

b. reference resources, including;
   i. how to search reference resources;
   ii. how to incorporate the use of reference resources into teaching.

13

Trainees must demonstrate in relation to the subject and age(s) of pupils to be taught that they:

a. **know how to use ICT to find things out**, including, as appropriate for the subjects and the age of pupils to be taught:
   i. identifying sources of information and discriminating between them;
   ii. planning and putting together a search strategy, including framing useful questions, widening and narrowing down searches;
   iii. how to search for information, including using key words and strings and logical operators such as AND, OR and NOT, indexes and directories;
   iv. collecting and structuring data and storing it for later retrieval, interpretation and correction;
   v. interpreting what is retrieved;
   vi. considering validity, reliability and reasonableness of outcomes;

b. **know how to use ICT to try things out, make things happen and understand how they happen** as appropriate for the subject(s) and the age of pupils to be taught:
   i. exploring alternatives;
   ii. modelling relationships;
   iii. considering cause and effect;
   iv. predicting patterns and rules recognising patterns, and hypothesising;

c. **know how to use ICT to communicate and exchange ideas** as appropriate to the subject(s) and the age of pupils to be taught:
   i. presenting ideas, including: identification of audience and purpose; deciding the best means with which to communicate;
   ii. exchanging ideas, including identifying the most appropriate medium, and information.

A computer can search through vast quantities of information, rapidly finding specific items, or a group of items that match an enquiry. Computers offer the pupil an opportunity for investigation and discovery of information from sources far beyond the scale available in the normal school library.

Pupils not only develop their subject knowledge but also the skills needed to deal with the speed and flexibility of information retrieval.

Sources of information

To search for information with a computer it has to have a database such as *Microsoft Access* or *Information Workshop* into which pupils or teachers have entered their own data. Alternatively it could be a commercial database with data-files, e.g. *Key Plus*.

CD-ROMs are also used as a source of information in many classrooms. Multimedia CD-ROMs enable pupils to browse through enormous quantities of information, including text, images, movies and sounds. To use a CD-ROM the computer needs a CD drive and the capability to play sounds. The Internet provides data on virtually any subject. Searching the Internet requires the computer to be on-line and equipped with a suitable Web browser.

Computer-based research

A feature of computers is their ability to store information for subsequent examination. They can also be used to compare quickly and test relationships between aspects of the information. They can find specific items of information, or a group of items that match an enquiry.

The results of a pupil's investigation will be given life through sharing what has been discovered with others: the ability to present results is also an important concept for a pupil to develop.

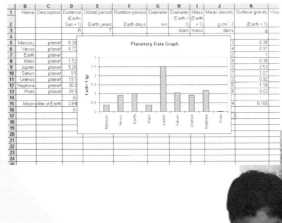

How to use IT

When set an appropriate task, pupils should be able to work independently, or as a team, to present their findings.

Effective research is a planned activity, so the pupils will have to:

* decide what they want to know and why
* decide how they will go about finding it
* plan how to record and organise the information discovered.

How not to use IT

The sheer quantity and opportunity for time-wasting demands that pupils develop disciplined research skills. Because pupils like 'discovery' activity they can become so enthralled with searching through a CD-ROM or the Internet that learning objectives are lost.

Teachers have to devise a system to ensure that while pupils are learning about the set topic they are also being taught to clarify what they are searching for, to follow links from one source to another and to drop leads that are a dead end.

Questions for pupils

* What are the advantages and disadvantages of using computer-based research compared to using books?
* How can we be sure the information discovered is accurate?
* How can we speed up our research?

Teachers will need to decide:

* what questions to ask
* how pupils will refine their searches to find only the information they need.

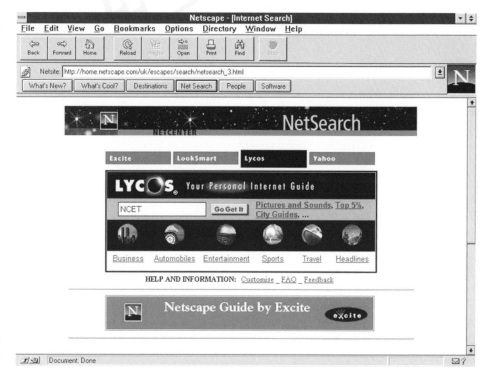

Pupils can explore information to seek patterns or individual answers to their searching. They might just be looking for an answer to a simple question such as 'when did...?', or they could be building a presentation on a specific subject that could include text, images and sounds.

The Internet creates a completely new opportunity for investigating and researching, but brings with it an even more acute need for research skills. Quite often investigating databases leads to the need to refine the questions being asked, to find other sources of information and to re-consider the anticipated outcomes.

The results of an investigation can lead to discussion about the most appropriate way to display the findings, taking into account the prospective audience and purpose. This may lead to the use of other computer programs.

Evaluating information

Information from the Internet can come from any source. The pages might be written by world authorities on a subject, or by pupils from another school. The variable status of the information is something that pupils will need to understand as their information skills develop.

CD-ROMs, like encyclopedias, are expensive to replace, so can easily become out of date. This emphasises the need, as in all research, of teaching how to judge if information is accurate.

Further information

Objectives in the use of ICT
Using database software
Using the Internet
Communicating information

Standards

13

Trainees must demonstrate in relation to the subject and age(s) of pupils to be taught that they:

b. know how to use ICT to try things out, make things happen and understand how they happen as appropriate for the subject(s) and the age of pupils to be taught:

   i. exploring alternatives;

   ii. modelling relationships;

   iii. considering cause and effect;

   iv. predicting patterns and rules recognising patterns, and hypothesising:

   v. knowing how to give instructions;

   vi. sequencing actions;

   vii. defining conditions e.g."if this happens, do that..";

   viii. understanding how feedback works and the difference between things that do and do not rely on feedback;e.g. knowing the importance of the grammar and syntax of instructions in ICT;

'Control' work is ultimately about the sequencing of instructions to make something behave in a particular way. At the higher levels this involves developing pupils' concepts of systemic thinking, such as analysing the inputs and outputs of systems and open and closed loop feedback systems.
ICT has much to offer the delivery of this type of work in schools.

In control?

Our everyday life seems to revolve around automatic devices: our kettles turn themselves off when the water boils, washing machines, video recorders and microwave ovens all work automatically. Even when we are outdoors our driving is controlled by traffic lights. We don't have to know how these devices work, and quite often we only know how to use some of the functions of the more complicated ones.

Quite apart from appreciating the implications of control on our lives, investigating and experimenting with control technologies leads pupils to develop a range of important cognitive skills. For young or inexperienced pupils control work encourages directional language such as forwards, backwards, and right and left turn, spatial awareness and the ability to estimate distance and turn. The more sophisticated pupil will find opportunities to develop high level problem-solving skills.

Making things happen

The essence of control work is the sequencing of instructions. Pupils have to break down the desired action into component steps, work out a sequence, and modify this in the light of their trials. Developing the ability to clarify a sequence of events is an important aim throughout the curriculum: control work provides an opportunity for teaching this skill in a way that pupils find exciting and relevant.

Pupils are able to control simple devices, for example a small robot or a Lego model, to follow a sequence of instructions. The least sophisticated application of control might be for one pupil to give direct instructions to another, such as 'walk one step forwards', 'turn right'. The most sophisticated applications will not only control a device, but will alter the actions in response to their external environment. A fan could turn on to cool a room, or a heater could be controlled to maintain a stable temperature in a model greenhouse: in these cases the sequence of actions would depend upon the signals provided by a temperature sensor.

To develop control work the teacher will need a simple programmable device to introduce the concepts. A floor turtle can be used as a starting point. This can be extended to working with a screen control language such as *Logo*. Later pupils can use programmable controllers (e.g., Lego Dacta systems), or an 'Interface' connected to a computer that in turn is connected to lights, motors and temperature or other sensors (e.g. 'Smart' boxes or Lego Control Lab). Using this technology pupils can model 'real-life' systems such as a production line or an automatic greenhouse.

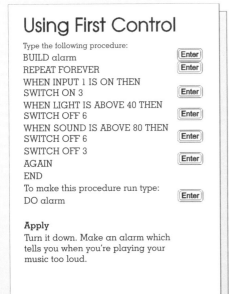

Using First Control

Type the following procedure:
BUILD alarm `Enter`
REPEAT FOREVER `Enter`
WHEN INPUT 1 IS ON THEN
SWITCH ON 3 `Enter`
WHEN LIGHT IS ABOVE 40 THEN
SWITCH OFF 6 `Enter`
WHEN SOUND IS ABOVE 80 THEN
SWITCH OFF 6 `Enter`
SWITCH OFF 3 `Enter`
AGAIN
END
To make this procedure run type:
DO alarm `Enter`

Apply
Turn it down. Make an alarm which tells you when you're playing your music too loud.

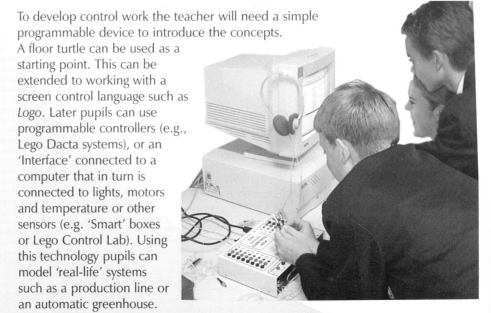

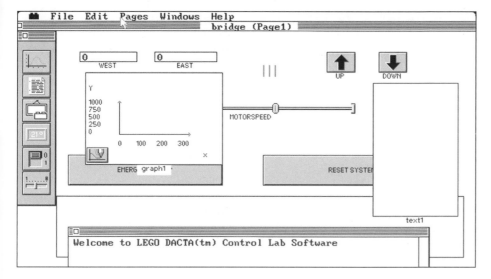

In practice

Control work motivates pupils and they are usually willing to persevere to clarify and develop their sequence of instructions until they get the outcomes they desire.

A perceived problem with control work in schools is that it conjures up an image of a complex tangle of wires and an equally complex computer program. The work seems abstract and pointless. By following a progression of teaching, using appropriate resources, these problems do not arise.

Because the result of their sequencing is a tangible action (movement of a floor turtle, a light going on or a motor turning) there is immediate feedback of results: pupils can see if things go wrong and are able to evaluate their sequence of instructions. By breaking down the task into its component parts and investigating the sequence pupils are developing a capability that is common to much of the work carried out in schools.

Control work can be used as a motivating teaching tool in many subjects. Pupils can combine control work with the design of models and they will be further developing the skills of decision-making into their sequences of instruction, especially when they are using sensors and feedback.

In Music the use of synthesisers, with or without computer editing programs, and digital systems such as MIDI interfaces are also control devices. These enable pupils to create, appraise, refine and control a range and sequence of sounds captured from acoustic instruments or created electronically.

When to use IT
When it allows pupils to
- develop numeracy skills
- understand the need for accuracy in framing instructions
- develop problem solving skills.

When not to use IT
When pupils cannot explore the way in which changing elements of the sequence affects the outcome.

What should a teacher know?
Can the teacher:
- connect an interface to a computer?
- run the software to control the interface?
- suggest a range of classroom applications in Geography, Science, English, Maths, D&T, Music?

Control in the curriculum
Control work has been strongly linked to D&T because the earliest applications in school were to control models. Sequencing is a common basic skill that is not confined to D&T.

Electronic music systems use control extensively in composition.

Modelling is closely related to the use of control applications once pupils begin to create their own control sequences.

Mathematics uses Logo and programmable vehicles to teach spatial concepts, angle, number and sequencing.

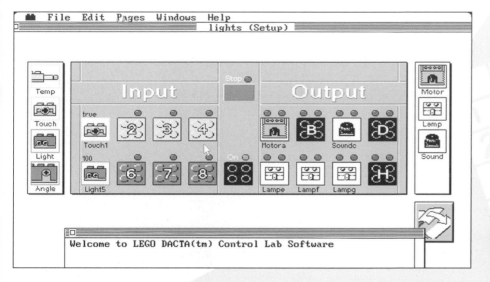

Further Information
The benefits of ICT in subject teaching
SEN and ICT
ICT in Mathematics
ICT in Music
Automatic functions (2): Sensing

Using ICT

Standards

14

Trainees must demonstrate that they know those features of ICT which can be used, separately or together, to support teaching and learning in subjects, including:

a. **speed and automatic functions** - the function of ICT which enables routine tasks to be completed and repeated quickly, allowing the user to concentrate on thinking and on tasks such as analysing and looking for patterns within data, asking questions and looking for answers, and explaining and presenting results, as appropriate to the subject(s) and age of pupils being taught, including how ICT can be used to:

   i. measure events at long or short time intervals in order to compress or expand events which would normally take very short or long periods of time, and illustrate them to pupils at speeds appropriate to their pace of learning;

   ii. measure and record events which might otherwise be impossible to gather within a classroom environment;

   iii. explore sequences of actions and link the sensing of events with the control of actions.

One of the useful automatic functions that computers can be made to perform is measuring changes in the environment using electronic sensors. This is usually called sensing or datalogging.

Computers offer teachers and pupils the opportunity to gather data which can then be processed to produce graphs and tables directly in the datalogging software or exported to a spreadsheet.

It is possible to arrange sensors to monitor changes in the environment and to feed the signals into a computer. For example, pupils could graph the changes in oxygen levels and temperature when pondweed is left on the surface of a container for a few days (long time intervals) or timing the acceleration of a falling object due to gravity (short time intervals). In Geography fieldwork pupils can collect data on stream-flow or on their oxygen pH and temperature.

To undertake sensing in the laboratory, classroom or in the field, teachers need access to:
- electronic sensors capable of being linked into an interface
- an interface or buffer box which links to the computer
- suitable software to aid analysis of the data that is collected.

For recording in the field a remote recorder is often referred to as a 'remote logger'. Remote loggers are devices which can operate without always being connected up to a computer. Typical systems have names such as DL PLUS, EMU, and LogIT. These are available in most secondary science departments. Sensing devices may be set up as weather stations in Geography.

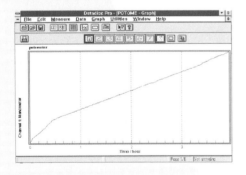

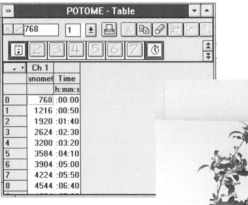

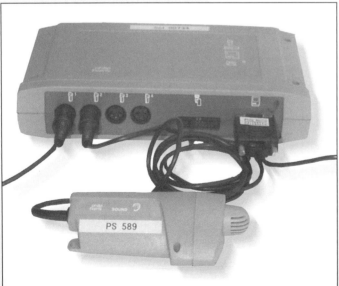

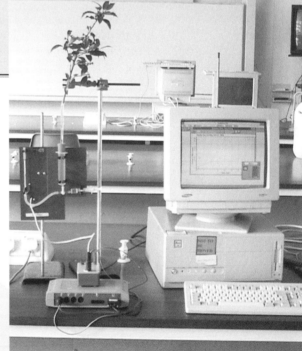

When to use IT

For collecting data that would be impossible or very difficult to do in any other way. The advantage of using these systems, over conventional recording systems, is that they can take hundreds of readings over many hours or days or very rapidly within a second, e.g. using a pressure sensor as part of a weather station to record rainfall over a month.

When not to use IT

- When lesson objectives identify pupils gaining basic skills with other measuring instruments, e.g. a thermometer.
- When it adds little to the pupils' experience or learning, i.e. the readings taken with conventional equipment are perfectly informative.
- When using sensing takes the experience out of the pupil's domain (if it replaces a good practical with a demonstration).

What should a teacher know?

Can the teacher:
- operate at least two different systems?
- handle a range of sensors?
- connect an interface to the computer?
- run the software to collect and process the data?
- suggest a range of classroom applications in Science, Geography or Physical Education?

Questions for pupils

- What are the advantages in using automatic data-gathering tools over traditional measuring instruments?
- Are electronic sensing systems more accurate than traditional methods?
- What are some of the best uses for automatic data-capture to be found in our society?
- Is all automatic data-capture advantageous to you as a citizen? Can automatic data gathering be a challenge to your personal privacy?

Sensing can change pupils' attitudes to practical science. Often thought of as 'more trouble than its worth!' sensing can offer even the lowest ability pupils an opportunity to achieve. On a user-friendly display, pupils can see instantly the results of their experiment evolving in real time.

Sensing software takes the effort out of graph-plotting. The instant feedback allows pupils to discuss the results between themselves and with the teacher without a de-motivating wait imposed by traditional paper methods of displaying data. The demands to evaluate and conclude in Sc1 stretch the most able and these are usually areas where achievement is lowest. Strategies which allow all pupils to interact more effectively with data will enhance their chances of achieving higher grades.

The ease of collecting subsequent readings from a re-run of an experiment encourages pupils to appreciate experimental errors. For example, an 'acceleration due to gravity' reading will rarely produce 9.81 ms^{-2}, but ten readings will illustrate the spread of readings and an average is likely to be usefully close to the accepted value.

Pupils are far more motivated to change variables and see the results. They are far more likely to make predictions if the data gathering is painless. Sensing makes asking 'what if?' questions more likely and possible for the pupils. for example, 'If I doubled the amount of insulation would it take twice as long to cool down?'

Further information

The benefits of ICT in subject teaching
ICT in Science
ICT in Geography
ICT in Physical Education

Standards

13

Trainees must demonstrate in relation to the subject and age(s) of pupils to be taught that they:

b. know how to use ICT to try things out, make things happen and understand how they happen as appropriate for the subject(s) and the age of pupils to be taught:
  i. exploring alternatives;
  ii. modelling relationships;
  iii. considering cause and effect;
  iv. predicting patterns and rules recognising patterns, and hypothesising;
  v. knowing how to give instructions;
  vi. sequencing actions;
  vii. defining conditions e.g."if this happens, do that..";
  viii. understanding how feedback works and the difference between things that do and do not rely on feedback.

'Computer models are, representations of the real world, or abstract situations... pupils should use, investigate, manipulate and later design, these models.'

NCC 1990 (NSG)

Modelling is an activity that many curriculum subjects share, from Science and Geography to Design and Technology and English. ICT resources offer a stimulating environment in which pupils can learn to manipulate pre-prepared models and then to construct their own. Simulations are just one aspect of modelling.

What is modelling?

Computer models can represent real or imagined situations. They are governed by rules and managed by the computer. They allow us to ask 'what would happen if...?' questions and to see what happens when changes are made. Modelling can use specific software such as a simulation or a computer-aided design (CAD) package. Alternatively, generic software such as a spreadsheet can be made to represent the situation through a set of mathematical relationships, for example, investigating the flight of a ball by changing a variable such as the angle of the throw.

Why is modelling useful?

Children are natural modellers of situations as, through play, they begin to make sense of their world. A computer can be used to broaden this experience. Modelling helps pupils to see the relationship between cause and effect and encourages logical, sequential and creative thought. Activities based on modelling are often of a collaborative nature. In exploring and explaining their thoughts with the rest of the group, pupils will analyse what they are doing and consolidate their learning. Solving simple problems through early modelling develops the ability pupils will need later to visualise and solve abstract problems. The power of modelling lies in its ability to allow pupils to say 'what would happen if...?' from a safe position.

Developing 'modelling capability'

The development of capability in modelling is likely to have two stages:

Teaching modelling

John Ogborn at the London Institute has explored the teaching of modelling using IT. To move pupils' modelling skills forward, he identified some of the skills pupils will need to model real situations.

- *identify the variables for a situation, i.e. not confuse events or objects as quantities*
- *think qualitatively about the situation*
- *draw causal diagrams for a given situation*
- *formulate relevant relationships*
- *validate the model qualitatively and quantitatively*

These are intellectually demanding skills which are a challenge to teachers' and pupils' capability. The increased availability of computer-aided design with graphical presentation aids offers new possibilities for using visual, diagrammatic methods of teaching and presenting ideas. Information graphics such as graphs, charts, maps, diagrams communicate in a way that is spatial, rather than verbal or symbolic.

Pre-modelling activities

Pre-modelling activities introduce pupils to many of the features of using computer models without requiring them to have the knowledge and precision necessary to create a computer model. For example, investigating the heat loss from containers using sensing equipment, prior to experimenting with a spreadsheet model of heat loss in houses.

Computer modelling

This goes a stage further when pupils can identify the rules and understand how they operate them, change them or create the structure for their own model. For example, pupils can work with spreadsheets and Logo to explore and investigate within models of their own making.

Understanding modelling

The elements of modelling are:

- *Visualisation*: Attempt to represent, in a simplified form, a complex situation which has many factors acting upon it.
- *Variables*: inputs that can be changed.
- *Outcomes*: the end result of the processes.
- *Rules*: the ways in which the variables interact, these can be changed in a model.
- *Relationships*: these emerge from examination of the behaviour.
- *Prediction and hypothesis*: pupils should be able to make predictions about the outputs and suggest ways of testing their ideas.

Modelling in the National Curriculum

The National Curriculum for IT requires pupils to use, investigate, manipulate and, later, design computer models.

Key Stage 3

Pupils should be taught to:
- modify the rules and a data of a model and predict the effect of such changes;
- evaluate a computer model by comparing its behaviour with data gathered from a range of sources.

Computer modelling in the classroom

Spreadsheet – on the farm

Pupils are investigating crop rotation and the factors which affect crop growth. They use a spreadsheet, which their teacher has prepared, to investigate the growth of crops over three years. By trying different crops in different fields, over the three years, they begin to gain an understanding of some of the factors which affect crop yield.

In this case, since the rules have been set by the teacher, the pupils are using the model as a simulation. If they base their decisions on a demonstrated understanding of the rules, then they have shown that they can use IT to explore patterns and relationships, and make simple predictions about the consequences of their decision making.

Older or more experienced pupils could modify the data and rules by adapting the spreadsheet formulae. They could then run the model to explore the effects of changing the variables in the computer model.

- *The variables*: location, type of crop, weather.
- *The outcomes*: crop yield.
- *The rules*: they are the formulae in the spreadsheet.
- *The relationships*: e.g. weather in relation to crop yield.
- *Prediction and hypothesis*: they use knowledge gained through first-hand experiences to judge the best combination and sequence of crops over a three-year period.

Branching narratives

As part of their work on a story, pupils create a branching narrative which presents a series of choices for the reader. The narrative is written on a computer using a framework in a hypertext program, presentation software or with an overlay keyboard program.

The pupils experiment with different ways of linking elements of the narrative and with varying sequences of episodes. They then give the narrative to others to read and explore. Discussions between the readers and writers lead to further refinement of the narrative.

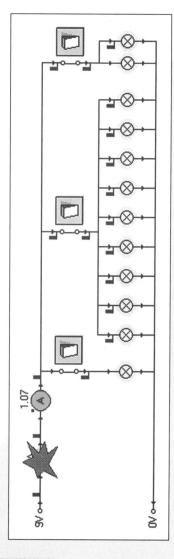

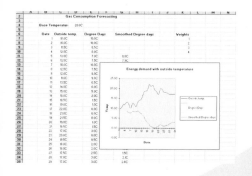

We would like to acknowledge the contribution of BECTa's *Information sheet: Modelling* to this page.

Using ICT

Standards

18.

Trainees must demonstrate that they are aware of:

a. the current health and safety legislation relating to the use of computers, and can identify potential hazards and minimise risks.

Every day we subject ourselves to potentially dangerous hazards. This is pertinent to the use of ICT within the classroom. Teachers will need to be aware of the current issues and health and safety legislation that exist and, along with common sense, they should be aware of how to minimise risks and to promote the safe use of IT in the classroom.

Current health and safety legislation

EC directives have set standards that cover the use of keyboards, software, desks, workstations, chair design and lighting. Developments in legislation for health and safety within the European Community led to the introduction of the *Management of Health and Safety at Work Regulations, 1992.* These regulations apply to '...an employee who habitually uses display screen equipment as a significant part of their normal work.' The *Electricity at Work Regulation, 1989* requires all electrical systems and equipment to be maintained in a safe condition.

There are two standards relating to the safety of IT equipment that the IT purchaser needs to be aware of:

- *The specification for safety of IT equipment including electrical business equipment (IEC/EN 60 950/BS 7002)*
- *Electrical systems in office furniture and office screens (BS 6396).*

Identifying potential risks

Over the last few years, there have been several issues that have caused concern over the habitual use of IT equipment. These include:

- repetitive strain injury (RSI)
- cumulative trauma disorder
- carpal tunnel syndrome
- tendinitis
- tenosynovitis
  - deQuervain's syndrome
  - thoracic outlet syndrome
  - computer eye syndrome or eye strain.

Much of the legislation is more applicable to administrative staff. Teachers have the overall responsibility to make sure that IT equipment is used correctly and safely. Where pupils are allowed to connect or unplug electrical equipment, this should be done under proper instruction and supervision by the teacher.

The positioning of equipment is very important, especially workstation design, which should enable users to reach all necessary equipment without stretching and should be clear of any obstruction.

Minimising risk

Ergonomics and good design of the working environment can help to overcome many health and safety problems, enabling people to work more effectively. This can be achieved in a number of ways.

- The work desk (or surface) should have a sufficiently large, low-reflective surface, and should have adequate space for the user to find a comfortable position.
- Chairs should be able to tilt, swivel and be adjustable.
- Users should have a foot rest, if required.
- Computer monitors should have anti-glare screens attached, if required.
- Computer monitors should be able to tilt and swivel.
- The keyboard should be tiltable and have a matt finish to avoid glare.
- There should be sufficient room to enable the mouse and a mat to be positioned alongside the keyboard.
- If using a laser printer, protective gloves or a vacuum cleaner with a special filter should be used when changing the toner cartridge. Modern laser printers have an ozone filter which should be changed regularly (consult the laser printer documentation for further advice).
- Circuit breakers should be used with all electrical equipment.
- The users should not spend more than 40 minutes in front of a computer; a 15 minute break is appropriate to relieve stress to the eyes.
- The room should be provided with adequate lighting.

Checklist

In particular, teachers should:
- check the lighting in a room
- provide alternative activities in long sessions
- be aware of any SEN problems which may be triggered by the monitors
- encourage good posture and positioning
- supervise pupils making hardware connections (avoid if possible).

Standards

18

Trainees must demonstrate that they are aware of:

b. legal considerations including those related to:
  i. keeping personal information on computers, as set out in the Data Protection Act;
  ii. copyright legislation relating to text, images and sounds and that related to copying software;
  iii. material which is illegal in this country

c. ethical issues including:
  i. access to illegal and/or unsuitable material through the Internet;
  ii. acknowledging sources;
  iii. data confidentiality;
  iv. the ways in which information sources can be (and are) monitored;
  v. material which may be socially or morally unacceptable.

Throughout the 1980s and '90s there has been a vast increase in the use of computers to access, store and process information. Alongside this growth there has been the development of new legislation and new measures to enact legislation with the aim of:

- *protecting an individual's right to privacy*
- *protecting an individual's intellectual property and copyright to any work that they have published electronically*
- *protecting individuals from exposure to obscene and inflammatory material.*

Data protection

The main purpose of the Data Protection Act of 1984 was to address concerns about the right to privacy of living persons. Teachers need to be aware of some of the more fundamental principles of the Act, particularly if they are planning to hold personal information on school computers. A new act will soon be in place.

Copyright

Copyright law is notoriously complex. Basically it exists to establish property rights of the creator or producer of an original work so that they may benefit from their efforts. A number of laws have been set up in an attempt to protect a person's property rights:

- The *Copyright, Designs and Patents Act 1988* makes it illegal for anyone to copy deliberately another person's work without their expressed permission.
- The *Copyright (Computer Programs) Regulations 1992* means that teachers have to seek permission or gain site licenses to make multiple copies of software.
- The *Computer Misuse Act 1990* makes it illegal for someone to gain access to a program or data held on a computer if they are not authorised to do so.

A person who creates, produces and stores text, images, video and sound clips on a computer is likely to be covered by copyright legislation. Though teachers, and their pupils, can invoke the law to protect their own information, they should be more concerned about violating copyright laws applying to computer programs and electronic information on the Internet.

Someone can only justifiably lay claim to something in a tangible form – thoughts cannot be considered property, but text, images, sound and computer software are tangible. It also has to be original – the product must be the result of intellectual effort. Facts cannot be subject to copyright law but the creativity employed to arrange them is, so creative editing of work may be a claim to copyright.

Copyright

Copyright provides automatic rights to the creators of the following kinds of material:

> (a) original literary works, e.g. novels, instruction manuals, computer programs, lyrics for songs, articles in newspapers, but **not** names or titles;
>
> (b) original dramatic works, including works of dance or mime;
>
> (c) original musical works;
>
> (d) original artistic works, e.g. paintings, engravings, photographs, sculptures, collages, works of architecture, technical drawings, diagrams, maps, logos;
>
> (e) published editions of works, i.e. the typographical arrangement of a publication;
>
> (f) sound recordings, which may be recordings on any medium, e.g. tape or compact disc, and may be recordings of other copyright works, e.g. musical or literary;
>
> (g) films, including videos; and
>
> (h) broadcasts and cable programmes.

Copyright does not protect ideas. Copyright may protect a work that expresses an idea but not the idea behind it.

Further information may be found on the following pages about copyright and related, unregistered intellectual property rights. However, the information does not amount to legal advice or opinion and carries no authority.

- Frequently asked questions
- Design right and protection for semiconductor chips
- Copyright and related rights policy: the Copyright Directorate
- Copyright and related rights news
- Copyright and related rights legislation
- The Copyright Tribunal

Related Areas

- Intellectual Property Policy Directorate

Home | patents | trade marks | designs | copyright | newcomer's guide | commercial searches | news and notices | intellectual property on the Internet | contact details | services | special projects

[Find] [Top]

nhv 1997

Pornography

Until a few years ago computer pornography had not been a major problem in schools. However, with the increase in home computer usage, the expansion of school computer facilities and the high profile that the issue gets in the media, it has raised considerable concerns by parents and teachers about pupils' access to computer pornography, particularly over the Internet.

The Obscene Publications Acts 1959 and 1964 help to identify offending authors and publicists of computer pornography but do not cover possession or transmission of the material, which are covered by other acts, such as the Criminal Justice Act 1988, the Criminal Justice and Public Order Act 1994, the Post Office Act 1953, the Telecommunications Act 1984 and the Public Order Act 1994. A combination of these acts covers most eventualities and the acts are a useful, if complex, reference.

Ethics

Schools would be advised to formulate their own set of ethical recommendations in order to convey to pupils the importance of an ethical approach to computing and the use of computers. Here are some pointers:

Unauthorised access (also known as 'hacking')

Ensure that networked or sensitive systems are password-protected and only given out on a need-to-know basis. Choose passwords that are hard to crack, e.g. don't use family or pet names as these can be guessed quite easily.

Acknowledge sources

When using someone else's work (text, pictures, sounds, etc) always seek permission to use it and acknowledge their right as the creator/producer of that work.

Data confidentiality

Ensure that personal data stored on computers has been registered with the Data Protection Registrar, and that absolute protection and confidentiality is maintained.

Unacceptable material

Ensure that pupils are aware that it is inappropriate to access and download material that is deemed obscene, inflammatory, or socially or morally unacceptable. Equally important, the school has a responsibility to prevent pupils accessing such materials. Software is available to prevent access to dubious sites.

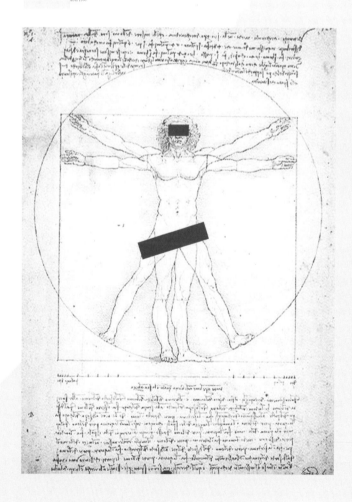

Standards

19

Trainees must demonstrate that they know how to use ICT to improve their own professional efficiency and to reduce administrative and bureaucratic burdens, including:

a. using ICT to aid administration, record-keeping, reporting and transfer of information;

b. knowing about current classroom-focused research and inspection evidence about the application of ICT to teaching their specialist subject(s), and where it can be found;

c. knowing how to use ICT to join in professional discussions and to locate and access teaching plans, material and other sources of help and support, including through the National Grid for Learning;

d. knowing how ICT can support them in their continuing professional development.

The use of ICT will play a key role in providing professional development for teachers. Schools will also increasingly use ICT to handle administrative and preparation work more efficiently.

Professional development with ICT

Staff development has traditionally relied on resources from a number of different sources:

- professional bodies, such as ASE for Science and NATE for English
- external courses run by the LEA or Higher Education Institutions
- supported self-study materials from organisations such as the Open University
- independent providers offering consultancy services as part of school development days.

On-line resources, provided via the Internet, to support curriculum and professional development are a recent development.

The National Grid for Learning (NGfL)

To support teachers' continued professional development the Government established the NGfL. This is an organised network of support agencies and resources which will be developed to meet the ICT needs of educational establishments, the workplace and homes. The NGfL will, it claims, be a resource for pupils and teachers where they can find on-line material to support teaching and learning. It is essentially a large Internet site providing access to a range of services.

Accessing on-line resources for staff development

From 1999 most schools will be connected to the Internet as part of a Government initiative to raise the profile of ICT in schools. The provision of new computers through which teachers can access staff development resources is one of the key strategies by which the Government proposes to train teachers. Schools are to be provided with a multimedia auditing tool which will identify teachers' training needs. The training will primarily be provided through access to training resources on the NGfL, i.e. on-line INSET. The grid is a very large archive of ideas and information on all curriculum subjects provided by teachers, organisations and commercial providers, and will be available to support combined professional development.

For staff working towards further professional qualifications or simply researching an area of professional practice there are library catalogues, on-line journals, information gateways and services, like the TES Library, that give access to archives, official documents and reports.

The Internet is also a means of delivering questionnaires which can reach a wide range of people quickly and effectively. Electronic forms are more appealing to fill in and submit than paper based ones!

On-line supported self-study modules or even whole Diploma and Masters courses are developing.

Access to inspection evidence and research

Professional subject bodies are still a source of information about effective use of ICT. In addition to their paper publications, many are now establishing a Web presence and are using this as a means of disseminating practice. OFSTED reports on schools are readily accessible. The DfEE provide most of their materials in an electronic format. The *Standards and Effectiveness* Database aims to be a central resource of data on the performance of schools which can be used to support school improvement. BECTa, operating within the NGfL, offer a large archive of research some of which is available on the Web site; others need to be accessed in printed form.

Teachers talking to teachers

The NGfL and providers such as The Times Educational Supplement, Schools On-line and Teachers On-line offer teachers the facility to exchange ideas, seek help on particular issues and develop their practice through professional dialogue using the Internet.

Using ICT to reduce administrative burdens

Documentation

Teaching has increasingly become a profession where the ability to handle administrative tasks efficiently is a vital part of performing effectively. The National Curriculum means that teachers need to have written schemes of work and school policy documents available for inspection by OFSTED. These need to be updated as the curriculum evolves and the school develops. The provisionality offered by word processors is the only way to manage the amendments without an undue amount of re-writing.

Assessment and record keeping

Keeping records of pupils' achievements means effective record keeping. Mark books work well to store marks and grades, but do not always yield the patterns of the performance of individuals or groups. ICT can help teachers see trends and patterns at an individual, class or year group level or compare one year with another. Spreadsheets are particularly useful to produce graphical information that teachers can use to plan the next step in terms of lessons or a scheme of work. Sorting grades or marks for analysis is simple with a spreadsheet. To save typing in names, class lists can be downloaded from the school management information system (MIS). Many schools have invested in computer-based assessment systems that can track the progress of a pupil throughout their time in school.

Presentation

Worksheets are useful for differentiation and support. Word processors and desk top publishing systems allow the teacher to produce worksheets that are aimed at different needs without the need to rewrite. Different font sizes, layout and illustration can all be added in a few minutes to adjust a presentation. If the pupils are using computers to present their work, templates can give structure and support to pupils who have organisational problems.

Publications

BECTa (1998) *The UK Integrated Learning Systems Evaluations: Final Report.*

NCET (1995) *Approaches to IT Capability: Key Stage 3.* NCET

DfEE (1995) *The National Curriculum. London HMSO*

DfEE (1998) *The National Literacy Strategy. London HMSO*

DfEE (1998) *Teaching: High Status, High Standards. Circular 4/98 London HMSO*

DfEE (1998) *The National Literacy Strategy:Framework for teaching. London HMSO*

World Wide Web Sites

DfEE
www.open.gov.uk/dfee

National Grid for Learning
www.ngfl.gov.uk

Virtual teacher centre (VTC)
www.vtc.ngfl.gov.uk

BECTa CD-ROM reviews
www.becta.org.uk/cd-rom.html

BECTa software reviews
www.becta.org.uk/publications/software/

BECTa information sheets
www.becta.org.uk/info-sheets/list.html

Special Needs Xplanatory.
www.cant.ac.uk/xplan.htm